Group's
Blockbuster
MOVIE ILLUSTRATIONS
THE RETURN

Bryan Belknap

Group
LOVELAND, COLORADO
group.com

Group resources actually work!

This Group resource incorporates our R.E.A.L. approach to ministry. It reinforces a growing friendship with Jesus, encourages long-term learning, and results in life transformation, because it's

Relational
Learner-to-learner interaction enhances learning and builds Christian friendships.

Experiential
What learners experience through discussion and action sticks with them up to 9 times longer than what they simply hear or read.

Applicable
The aim of Christian education is to equip learners to be both hearers and doers of God's Word.

Learner-based
Learners understand and retain more when the learning process takes into consideration how they learn best.

Group's Blockbuster Movie Illustrations: The Return
Copyright © 2006 Bryan Belknap

Visit out website: **group.com**

Credits
Acquisitions Editor: Kate S. Holburn
Assistant Editor: Amber Van Schooneveld
Creative Development Editor: Mikal Keefer
Chief Creative Officer: Joani Schultz
Copy Editor: Janis Sampson
Art Director: Nancy Serbus
Cover Art Director/Designer: Jeff Storm
Production Manager: DeAnne Lear

Library of Congress Cataloging-in-Publication Data
Belknap, Bryan.
    Group's blockbuster movie illustrations : the return / by Bryan Belknap.--
1st American pbk. ed.
        p. cm.
    Includes indexes.
    ISBN: 978-0-7644-2981-1 (alk. paper)
1. Motion pictures in Christian education. 2. Christian education of
teenagers. I. Group Publishing. II. Title.
    BV1535.4.B453 2006
    286' .67--dc22   2006001663

ISBN 978-0-7644-2981-1
10 9 8 7 6 5 4 3   15 14 13 12 11 10 09 08
Printed in the United States of America.

CONTENTS

Introduction
5

Movie Illustration Themes A–C
9-33

Movie Illustration Themes D–F
34-55

Movie Illustration Themes G–K
56-75

Movie Illustration Themes L–O
76-88

Movie Illustration Themes P-R
89-105

Movie Illustration Themes S-Z
106-130

Movie Background Index
131

Scripture Index
146

Topical Index
153

DEDICATION

Thanks go out to my editors Kate Holburn and
Amber Van Schooneveld for helping me sound eloquent,
and to my writing group (Go Overlords!) for pushing me
to glorify God with excellence.

I once again dedicate this to my biggest fan, Jill, for
supporting me every step of the way, and to our son,
Cash, who brings so much joy.

INTRODUCTION

Third time's a charm.

You hold in your hand the painstaking completion of a trilogy. (You missed the first two books? You wouldn't watch *Return of the Jedi* first, would you? Get thee to a bookstore forthwith, and complete the set!)

All kidding aside, much has changed since I started writing *Group's Blockbuster Movie Illustrations* five years ago. Back in the 20th century (how quaint!), I had to convince ministers of the benefits that come from using video clips to illustrate biblical truth.

Fast forward to the present where even "big church" frequently uses clips. (Sometimes *too* frequently. Do we really need a video clip during the potluck after the service?) It's been a wonderful thing for me to hear from youth workers around the country whose students complain they've been "ruined" for life—unable to watch movies without relating it to their faith.

I continue to ruin this generation with pride.

All this is to say that movie clip illustrations *work!* They not only put some flesh, context, and relevance to the Bible's eternal truths, but movie clips also train young people to shove every Hollywood nugget they ingest through their "Jesus filter," chewing on the spiritual meat while flushing any cruddy gristle down the disposal.

Thus, we had to complete the trilogy. Lots of great things come in threes. Reese's peanut butter cups. Larry, Moe, and Curly. The Godfather series. (Actually, the third movie was mediocre, but you get the analogy.) As with any successful sequel, everything's bigger and better. More illustrations—over 175. Bigger hit films—*Bruce Almighty, The Lord of the Rings: The Return of the King, Napoleon Dynamite, Spider-Man 2*. I even throw in some classics for extra spice—*Armageddon, Mrs. Doubtfire, The Apostle*. We've also added the DVD chapter information so you can jump straight to the scene you want.

All in all, this edition will surpass what you've come to know and love about *Group's Blockbuster Movie Illustrations*. (And don't forget to find even more unique clips on www.ministryandmedia.com. Check it out!)

Thank you for making this series successful. I pray these illustrations draw those you lead into a deeper relationship with their loving Savior. God bless your ministry!

How to Use *Group's Blockbuster Movie Illustrations: The Return*

Remember, it's not about the video clip. You're concerned with communicating the life-changing truth of God. You don't need to give a movie's title, rating, or summary. Use the clip to capture attention or get a conversation started, and then forget it—focus on the Word of God.

***Content**—*Before you dive into showing video clips at church, *preview them!* All clips presented in this book are completely acceptable in content to most people. Some church-specific inappropriate behavior, such as dancing or drinking alcohol may appear. Note: Only two clips carry an R rating. Both come from *The Passion of the Christ* and were included due to the film's tremendous impact on Christian audiences around the world. For appropriate clips from other R-rated films, go to www.ministryandmedia. com.

Also, we do not guarantee the content before or after the suggested clip. You *must* know when to turn the VCR or DVD player on and off so you do not spend your entire meeting apologizing for a mistake. (Beware: Some VCRs roll back five to 10 seconds when stopped. Yet another reason to splurge the $50 for a DVD player, you miser!) So you can be on the alert, we've added a warning whenever questionable material occurs soon before or after a clip.

***Copyright Laws**—*To comply with copyright laws, a few simple rules should be followed. Though clips under three minutes (like the ones included in this book) are technically covered under the fair use doctrine (which allows portions of a work to be exhibited for educational purposes), it's better to be safe than sued. You can obtain a blanket licensing agreement from CVLI, much like your church's CCLIC agreement for music. Visit www.cvli.org for more information. That said, you *cannot* charge admission to a function where you screen either clips or entire movies, license or not. As a purely practical note, we don't recommend screening clips longer than three minutes simply because the focus shifts from parable into entertainment viewing.

***Parents**—*It's a good idea to send students home with a permission slip before you start showing movie clips. You don't need anything fancy or written in blood—a simple "Here's what's up" should suffice. Parents just need to know you haven't joined the cult of cinema. Try something like:

Jesus taught deep spiritual truth with examples from everyday life. The modern parallel to Jesus' parables is film. In an effort to connect teenagers' everyday life with their faith while illustrating spiritual matters in a concrete way they will grasp, I would like to use movie clips as illustrations during our youth events.

Every clip is carefully screened and contains no objectionable content. The clips will be three minutes or less so the focus always remains on God's Word and never the movie itself. My prayer is to bring Scripture alive and get your young people thinking about their faith outside the church walls by using these clips.

Please contact me with any questions or concerns about showing movie clips in the youth ministry. Please sign below if you have no objections. Thank you for your time and your trust with your child's spiritual growth!

To make your job easier, each movie illustration is presented in the following way:

Theme | THEME SUBTITLE

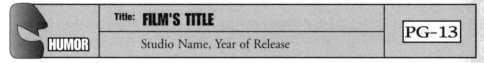

	Title: **FILM'S TITLE**	
HUMOR	Studio Name, Year of Release	**PG-13**

Theme—The theme of the clip, such as purity, grace, or honesty.

Humor/Drama Icon—These icons at the beginning of each illustration let you know if the tone of the clip is humorous or dramatic.

Title—The film's title, studio, year of release, and rating.

Scripture—The Scripture passage that relates to the clip's theme.

Alternate Takes—Each of the clips in this book could be used to spark many different discussions. So we've included alternate themes and Scriptures that can be used with the same clip.

DVD Chapter—The chapter in which the clip takes place, so you can skip right to it.

Start Time/End Time—These times tell you when to start and stop the film. They are organized in hours, minutes, and seconds, and are rounded to the closest 15-second interval. If you are using a VCR, clip locations are determined by setting your tape counter to 00:00:00 when the studio logo for the film appears immediately before the opening credits.

Start Cue/End Cue—These visual and audio cues will let you know exactly when the clip begins and ends. As the start and end times are approximated to the nearest 15-second interval, it's a good idea to read these cues so you know you're at just the right spot.

Duration—This is the elapsed time for the clip. We've kept them short— under three minutes—to keep the focus in the right place.

Overview—Here you'll find a description of the scene's action and the characters' names. For an overview of the plot of the movie itself, see the Movie Background Index in the back of the book.

Illustration—Use this short explanation of how the clip relates to Scripture and the 21st-century teen experience as a jumping-off point for exploration of spiritual themes.

Questions—These questions will get your discussions really going and help kids apply the truths from the illustrations to their lives.

We've also included several easy-to-use indexes:

Movie Background—This section provides a brief overview of the entire movie. You can look informed even if you haven't seen the whole movie! For greater depth, search for the movie at www.imdb.com, which gives brief summaries of the movies' plots.

Scripture Index—For those looking for a clip to illustrate the sermon you've prepared, simply find your focus Scripture and go from there!

Topical Index—If you're giving a talk on faith in five minutes and need an attention-grabbing film clip, this index is for you.

MOVIE ILLUSTRATION THEMES

Abortion | IT WILL HAUNT YOU

DRAMA	**Title: CATCH ME IF YOU CAN** DreamWorks, 2002	**PG-13**

Scripture: Psalm 139:13-16
Alternate Take: Discipline (Proverbs 13:24)

DVD CHAPTER:	13
START TIME:	1 hour, 20 minutes, 00 seconds
START CUE:	Frank and Brenda lie in bed.
END TIME:	1 hour, 21 minutes, 45 seconds
END CUE:	Frank says, "I asked permission to marry you.
DURATION:	1 minute, 45 seconds

Overview: Brenda confesses to having had an abortion and getting kicked out of her house. Frank asks if they'd take her back if she was engaged to him.

Warning: *Frank and Brenda are in their undergarments in bed in this scene. The scene is tastefully done, but you may want to beware for younger viewers.*

Illustration: Abortion brings great sorrow to those involved as well as to God. Correct any misconceptions among your students about this "option" while offering hope and God's forgiveness to any who bear the guilt of this poor choice.

Questions:
- **What is your opinion on abortion?**
- **Do you think the debate over abortion will ever end? Why or why not?**
- Read Psalm 139:13-16. **Why do Christians often cite this verse as evidence for the sanctity of life? Do you agree? Explain.**
- **Does God forgive someone who has had an abortion? Why or why not?**
- **What are some practical, loving things Christians can do to curb the number of abortions performed each year?**

Absent Father | WHERE IS HE?

DRAMA	**Title: WHAT A GIRL WANTS** Warner Brothers, 2003	**PG**

Scripture: Romans 8:14-17
Alternate Take: God's Love (1 John 4:16-19)

DVD CHAPTER:	2
START TIME:	8 minutes, 45 seconds
START CUE:	Kids run down a hill.
END TIME:	10 minutes, 15 seconds
END CUE:	Mom kisses Daphne's forehead.
DURATION:	1 minute, 30 seconds

Overview: Daphne's upset because she'll never have a father-daughter dance at her wedding. She wants to meet him because she feels a part of her is missing, but Mom says Daphne only needs to know herself.

Illustration: God places in us an innate need to connect with our earthly fathers. Unfortunately, far too many people either don't know their dads or have dads who are not interested in knowing them. Help your students bond with the heavenly Father who fills in these gaps with his perfect Spirit.

Questions:
- **How would you describe your relationship with your father?**
- **What one thing could your father do to make your relationship with him better?**
- Read Romans 8:14-17. **How can a heavenly, invisible God possibly fill in for the deficiencies of your earthly father?**
- **Have you ever felt God's fatherly presence in your life? If so, explain.**
- **How will you pray for an improved relationship with both your heavenly and your earthly father?**

Absolute Truth | WHAT IS TRUTH?

Title: **THE PASSION OF THE CHRIST**	
DRAMA	New Market Films, 2004	R

Scripture: Matthew 7:24-29

Alternate Takes: Discernment (Philippians 1:9-10), Responsibility (Leviticus 5:17)

DVD CHAPTER:	14
START TIME:	46 minutes, 15 seconds
START CUE:	Claudia enters the room.
END TIME:	47 minutes, 45 seconds
END CUE:	A soldier shouts from off screen.
DURATION:	1 minute, 30 seconds

Overview: Pilate asks Claudia, "What is truth?" He wants to know how she recognizes it. Claudia believes a person who won't hear it will never receive it. Pilate retorts that the truth is he'll be responsible for Jesus' bloodshed no matter which way he turns.

Illustration: Seems like everybody's asking Pilate's question about truth these days. What was universally accepted has now become a battlefield over competing ideas and worldviews. Give your youth the firm foundation of God's absolute truth—not to bludgeon others with, but as a firm foundation for themselves.

Questions:
- **How would you answer Pilate's question, "What is truth?"**
- **Why do people have such divergent opinions about truth these days?**
- **What positive effect does this confusion have on our culture? What negative effect?**

- Read Matthew 7:24-29. **How can Jesus make the claim that his words remain firm (or true) while all others wash away?**
- **How would trusting the words in the Bible as absolute truth bring stability to your life? What's stopping you from doing that?**

Abuse | DON'T ACCEPT IT

DRAMA	Title: **THE RAINMAKER** Paramount Pictures, 1997	PG-13

Scripture: Exodus 3:7-9
Alternate Take: Righteous Anger (Ephesians 4:25-27)

DVD CHAPTER:	7
START TIME:	29 minutes, 30 seconds
START CUE:	Rudy closes the door.
END TIME:	31 minutes, 30 seconds
END CUE:	Rudy says, "That's not gonna happen."
DURATION:	2 minutes

Overview: Rudy tells Kelly that any man who beats his wife should be shot. She should file for divorce and flee before her husband beats her to death. Unfortunately, Kelly's too scared to leave him.

Illustration: Abuse—physical, verbal, sexual—is the dirty little secret happening in far too many homes. Remind your students they don't have to suffer in silence and solitude, but they can find help and healing from their situations.

Questions:
- **Why would anyone remain in such a terrible situation?**
- **What are some other forms of abuse that you've heard of?**
- Read Exodus 3:7-9. **Why didn't God immediately rescue the Israelites from their suffering?**
- **How can God bring comfort to a person in the midst of any abuse he or she might be experiencing?**
- **How can we help people escape abusive situations?**

Accountability | YOUR PROBLEM IS MY PROBLEM

DRAMA	Title: **DRUMLINE** 20th Century Fox, 2002	PG-13

Scripture: Proverbs 27:6-9
Alternate Take: Teamwork (Hebrews 10:32-36)

DVD CHAPTER:	4
START TIME:	11 minutes, 00 seconds

START CUE:	Dr.. Lee says, "Good morning."
END TIME:	13 minutes, 30 seconds
END CUE:	The band runs laps.
DURATION:	2 minutes, 30 seconds

Overview: Dr. Lee preaches the virtues of teamwork. He asks a latecomer the name of his roommate. Dr. Lee turns to the roommate, Devon, asking why he didn't wake up his roomie who overslept. Devon replies that he's not a mother. Dr.. Lee proclaims that one late person means they're all late. They must watch out for each other.

Illustration: We share a portion of the responsibility when a brother or sister in the faith falls. Discuss true accountability with your young people—where they can find it, what it involves, and how it will protect them from stumbling.

Questions:

- **Do you think Dr.. Lee was being fair? Why or why not?**
- **Are we responsible for our Christian brothers and sisters when they stumble or fall in their faith? Explain.**
- Read Proverbs 27:6-9. **What advice do these verses give concerning accountability?**
- **What ingredients create an open, honest relationship in which someone can lovingly challenge your actions and faith?**
- **Why is it important to be accountable to someone? What's stopping you from that kind of accountability?**

Addiction | I CAN HANDLE IT

DRAMA	Title: **MINORITY REPORT**	
	20th Century Fox, 2002	PG-13

Scripture: Philippians 3:17-21

Alternate Take: Grief (Isaiah 35:4-10)

DVD CHAPTER:	3
START TIME:	18 minutes, 00 seconds
START CUE:	John picks a slide.
END TIME:	20 minutes, 00 seconds
END CUE	John slumps back in a chair.
DURATION:	2 minutes

Overview: John watches a video of himself teaching his small son how to run. His son was kidnapped and never found. After watching the video, he takes a hit from some drugs to ease his painful memories.

Illustration: People have lots of reasons for taking addictive substances, but they always fail to find the answers they seek. Warn your students of the physical and spiritual dangers associated with any type of addiction.

Questions:

- What are some reasons people have for becoming addicted to something?
- At what point does someone become addicted?
- What kinds of things, besides drugs, might a person become addicted to?
- Read Philippians 3:17-21. **How does an addiction control a person's physical life? spiritual life?**
- What can we do to help someone break an addiction?

Anger | DON'T MAKE ME ANGRY

| | **Title: HULK** | **PG-13** |
| DRAMA | Universal Pictures, 2003 | |

Scripture: Proverbs 15:18
Alternate Take: Self-Control (Proverbs 25:28)

DVD CHAPTER:	15
START TIME:	57 minutes, 45 seconds
START CUE:	Bruce says, "My father's going after Betty."
END TIME:	59 minutes, 15 seconds
END CUE:	Talbot hits the pavement.
DURATION:	1 minute, 30 seconds

Overview: Talbot pushes Bruce around, thinking he's getting cut out of the deal. Bruce warns him to stop, but Talbot won't listen. Bruce gets angry and transforms into the Hulk.

Illustration: Anger isn't necessarily a sin, but allowing it to erupt into Hulk-like proportions definitely is. Help your youth get a handle on their anger, learning to please God even when they see green.

Questions:

- When was the last time you got really angry?
- Did you glorify God in your anger? Why or why not?
- Read Proverbs 15:18. **Does this mean we can't defend ourselves when someone wrongs us? Why or why not?**
- How might curbing your anger in past situations have helped bring a more peaceful solution?
- How can a person learn to become "slow to anger"? (Proverbs 15:18, *New King James Version*)

Armor of God | GEAR UP

| | **Title: SPY KIDS 2: THE ISLAND OF LOST DREAMS** | **PG** |
| HUMOR | Dimension Films, 2002 | |

Scripture: Ephesians 6:11-17
Alternate Take: Creativity (Exodus 35:30–36:1)

DVD CHAPTER:	5
START TIME:	28 minutes, 00 seconds
START CUE:	The kids rappel from the ceiling.
END TIME:	29 minutes, 15 seconds
END CUE:	Carmen kicks the screen.
DURATION:	1 minute, 15 seconds

Overview: Machete gives the kids a lot of high-tech gear for their mission. He finishes with a simple rubber band. It has 999 uses and also works your mind—you have to figure the uses out. Carmen and Juni suit up.

Illustration: God has given his children armor to use in spiritual battle. Encourage your teens to don the important equipment he has given them.

Questions:
- **Do you think we as Christians do a good job preparing for the spiritual battle we face? Why or why not?**
- Read Ephesians 6:11-17. **Why doesn't God automatically put these things on us, instead asking us to do it?**
- **What prevents you from donning all your armor?**
- **What benefits would come from making every piece of armor a natural part of your life?**
- **Which piece of armor do you find the most difficult to put on? Why?**

Authenticity | WHITE MEN *CAN* DANCE

	Title: **HITCH**	
HUMOR	Columbia Pictures, 2005	PG-13

Scripture: Proverbs 13:5-7

Alternate Take: Dancing (Psalm 150:4-6)

DVD CHAPTER:	15
START TIME:	49 minutes, 30 seconds
START CUE:	DJ spins a record.
END TIME:	51 minutes, 00 seconds
END CUE:	Hitch says, "Don't need no pizza."
DURATION:	1 minute, 30 seconds

Overview: Albert assures Hitch that he's got great dance floor moves. He busts out some truly ridiculous steps, prompting Hitch to demonstrate exactly how Albert must dance in order to make a good impression.

Illustration: Everybody wants authenticity, but peer pressure, the need for acceptance, or flat out fear of rejection stifles it. Confidence and faith in God's beautifully and wonderfully made creation (that's you) allows authenticity to flourish in a person's life.

Questions:
- Have you ever changed or hidden something about yourself so you could impress others? If so, what happened?
- What prevents people from simply being themselves?
- Read Proverbs 13:5-7. Do you think these verses are too harsh? Why or why not?
- How does a lack of authenticity indicate a weak faith in God?
- Where do you need to be more authentic in your life, and how will you do that?

Authority | I COMMAND THEE, GET OUT!

	Title: **RAISING HELEN**	
HUMOR	Touchstone Pictures, 2004	PG-13

Scripture: 2 Timothy 1:6-7
Alternate Take: Confidence (Isaiah 41:8-10)

DVD CHAPTER:	7
START TIME:	54 minutes, 45 seconds
START CUE:	Jenny says, "What's that noise?"
END TIME:	56 minutes, 45 seconds
END CUE:	"Good night, Helen."
DURATION:	2 minutes

Overview: Audrey parties with friends in the living room. Helen timidly asks them to leave, but they ignore her. She asks Nilma to help, and the fiery woman grabs a baseball bat and chases the hooligans out.

Illustration: We don't need to walk around like wimps, cowering in the face of popular opinion. Challenge your young people to claim the authority they have in the name of Christ, standing strong in the face of opposition.

Questions:
- What emotions or beliefs make us timid about our authority in Christ?
- Read 2 Timothy 1:6-7. What authority do we have as children of God?
- Do you feel comfortable using that authority? Why or why not?
- How can a person learn to take the authority God has given every Christian in the face of opposition?

Belief | I CAN FLY!

	Title: **FINDING NEVERLAND**	
DRAMA	Miramax Films, 2004	PG

Scripture: Hebrews 11:1-13
Alternate Take: Faith (Matthew 17:20)

DVD CHAPTER:	2
START TIME:	10 minutes, 00 seconds
START CUE:	Barrie and his dog stare face to face.
END TIME:	12 minutes, 45 seconds
END CUE:	Barrie and the dog fall to the ground.
DURATION:	2 minutes, 45 seconds

Overview: Mr. Barrie says he will dance with an extremely dangerous bear. Peter points out that the "bear" is only a dog. Barrie reprimands his lack of faith. Anyone with imagination and belief can see the bear. As he dances with his dog, the boys "see" Barrie, dressed in a ringmaster's uniform, dancing with a bear in a circus.

Illustration: Sure, seeing is believing. But believing is also seeing. Without a "blind" step of faith, a person will struggle to see the face of God. When people put faith in what their senses can't corroborate, their ability to believe skyrockets.

Questions:
- **Do you relate more to Barrie or Peter in this scene? Why?**
- **What kinds of things do you find difficult to believe?**
- Read Hebrews 11:1-13. **Could you do what the men and women in these verses did? Explain.**
- **Why does God ask us to believe something before he gives proof?**
- **What is God asking you to believe, and what needs to happen for you to act on that belief?**

Betrayal | ET TU, BRUTE?

Title: **ROBIN HOOD: PRINCE OF THIEVES**	
HUMOR	Warner Brothers, 1991

PG-13

Scripture: Isaiah 33:1-2
Alternate Take: Judas (Mark 14:10-11)

DVD CHAPTER:	33
START TIME:	1 hour, 52 minutes, 00 seconds
START CUE:	The exterior of the castle is shown on the screen.
END TIME:	1 hour, 54 minutes, 00 seconds
END CUE:	Sheriff of Nottingham finishes, "...remove your lying tongue."
DURATION:	2 minutes

Overview: The sheriff enters the dungeon looking for information on Robin Hood. Will Scarlett offers to help because he hates Robin. He guarantees he can get close because Robin is a trusting fool.

Illustration: Betrayal stings deep and long. Discuss this nasty deed and how your youth can find healing from its touch.

Questions:

- Have you ever been betrayed? If so, what happened?
- What makes betrayal such a hurtful action?
- Read Isaiah 33:1-2. What promise does God give to people who betray? to people who are betrayed?
- What solace can a betrayed person take in these verses?
- What beliefs or attitudes do you need to purge from your life so you never betray another?

The Bible | IT'S NOT GOING ANYWHERE

DRAMA	Title: THE APOSTLE Universal Pictures, 1997	PG-13

Scripture: Luke 16:16-17
Alternate Takes: Church (Hebrews 10:23-25), Enemies (Luke 6:27-30)

DVD CHAPTER:	30
START TIME:	1 hour, 40 minutes, 15 seconds
START CUE:	A troublemaker says, "I told you I'd come back."
END TIME:	1 hour, 43 minutes, 15 seconds
END CUE:	Sonny kneels with the troublemaker.
DURATION:	3 minutes

Overview: A troublemaker rides up on a bulldozer ready to knock the church down. Sonny refuses to move, laying his Bible in front of the 'dozer, saying he won't drive over it. The troublemaker says he isn't scared, but he still can't move the Bible.

Illustration: People forget the physical and spiritual power of God's Word. Remind your young people that the Bible is not to be trifled with and that they can rely on its strength in their time of need.

Questions:

- Why couldn't the man run over the Bible?
- Read Luke 16:16-17. Why does the Bible have power, even with people who claim not to believe it?
- What are some ways we can use or receive power from Scripture?
- How can we use the power of Scripture to advance God's kingdom?

The Bible | IT'S SOLID

DRAMA	Title: SHATTERED GLASS Lions Gate Film, 2003	PG-13

Scripture: Revelation 22:16-19
Alternate Take: Cheating (Leviticus 6:1-5)

DVD CHAPTER:	13
START TIME:	48 minutes, 45 seconds
START CUE:	Stephen says, "I'd like to pause for a moment."
END TIME:	50 minutes, 45 seconds
END CUE:	Stephen ends, "...the notes provided by the reporter himself."
DURATION:	2 minutes

Overview: Stephen recounts the rigorous editing process every New Republic article endures before going to print. Despite all of the revisions and fact checking, writers can still slip in fabrications by faking their notes.

Illustration: The Bible has been interpreted to support almost anything under the sun through the centuries. Even today, people armed with a couple of verses sway those who are not grounded in Scripture to join their heresies. Teach your kids that God's entire Word is inerrant and must agree as a whole, not just in bits and pieces.

Questions:
- **Do you believe fabrications or mistakes made their way into the Bible? Explain.**
- **How does your position on that question affect how you approach your faith?**
- Read Revelation 22:16-19. **How can the author of Revelation claim that the Bible is perfect?**
- **If the Bible does have errors, how does a person discern which Scripture to live by and which Scripture to ignore?**

Body Image | I WANNA BE A SUPERMODEL

HUMOR	**Title:** **13 GOING ON 30**	
	Columbia Pictures, 2004	PG-13

Scripture: Psalm 139:13-16

Alternate Takes: Impatience (Psalm 37:5-7), Media Messages (1 Samuel 16:7), Contentment (1 Timothy 6:6-8)

DVD CHAPTER:	1
START TIME:	4 minutes, 45 seconds
START CUE:	Jenna applies makeup.
END TIME:	6 minutes, 00 seconds
END CUE:	Jenna stuffs her bra.
DURATION:	1 minute, 15 seconds

Overview: Jenna whines about how much she hates her body—she wants to look like the models in Poise magazine! Mom assures her she *will* some day, but right now she should be content as a beautiful 13-year-old girl. Mom leaves, and Jenna immediately stuffs her bra.

Illustration: Many of your students (male and female) probably struggle with body image. Take up the encouragement from Jenna's mother, and run with it. Poor body image can turn into doubt about God's love and make entering into Christian community difficult. Help instill in your youth a healthy body image based on the truth that they are "fearfully and wonderfully made."

Questions:

- If you could change one thing about your looks, what would it be and why?
- How does discontentment with your looks affect your self-esteem? your relationship with God?
- Read Psalm 139:13-16. Do you think God made a mistake when he made you? Why or why not?
- How much does a person's inner life affect their outward appearance?
- How can you learn to see yourself as "wonderfully made"?

The Body of Christ | YOU'RE THE PANCREAS

HUMOR	Title: **SCHOOL OF ROCK**	PG-13
	Paramount Pictures, 2003	

Scripture: 1 Corinthians 12:14-31

Alternate Takes: Community (Acts 2:42-47), Serving Others (1 Peter 4:10-11)

DVD CHAPTER:	6
START TIME:	29 minutes, 30 seconds
START CUE:	Kids stand lined up against the blackboard.
END TIME:	31 minutes, 00 seconds
END CUE:	Dewey says, "Sit down."
DURATION:	1 minute, 30 seconds

Overview: Dewey assigns everyone parts in the band, either as musicians, security, roadies, or fans. He states that everyone is needed to make the band great.

Illustration: God has placed each person in your church so it will function the way he intended. His divine purpose becomes hindered when both those behind the scenes and the "stars" on stage don't work together. Help identify each of your kids "bodily function," and then empower them to use it for God's glory.

Questions:

- How is being in a church similar to being part of the band Dewey set up?
- How would you feel if you weren't playing an instrument, but were a roadie or security person instead?
- Read 1 Corinthians 12:14-31. Why do you think God has brought you into this particular church body?
- What happens when someone isn't using his or her gifts or talents at church?
- How can you use your gifts or talents to improve our church "body"?

Boldness | DON'T HOLD BACK

Title: LEGALLY BLONDE 2: RED, WHITE & BLONDE	**PG-13**
HUMOR MGM, 2003	

Scripture: Acts 4:29-33

Alternate Takes: Participation (1 Corinthians 12:20-27),
Works (James 2:17-24)

DVD CHAPTER:	30
START TIME:	1 hour, 23 minutes, 15 seconds
START CUE:	Elle starts, "One day I came to Washington…"
END TIME:	1 hour, 26 minutes, 15 seconds
END CUE:	The crowd claps.
DURATION:	3 minutes

Overview: Elle addresses Congress on the importance of…her hair. She recounts going to an exclusive salon that fried her hair. She blames herself for not speaking up. You can't just watch injustice; you must speak up, stand up, and do something.

Illustration: We have the truth of almighty God on our lips, so there's no reason to hold back. Challenge your teens to join Elle in speaking boldly whenever the opportunity presents itself.

Questions:
- **Do you think you could stand up and speak what you believe with boldness like Elle? Why or why not?**
- Read Acts 4:29-33. **Do we have the same power as the apostles to speak as God's group? Explain.**
- **What obstacles prevent you from speaking the truth with boldness?**
- **How can you learn to become more bold about your faith?**

Bullies | GIMME YOUR LUNCH MONEY

Title: NAPOLEON DYNAMITE	**PG**
HUMOR Fox Searchlight, 2004	

Scripture: 1 John 3:16-18

Alternate Take: Helping Others (Luke 10:29-37)

DVD CHAPTER:	14
START TIME:	1 hour, 1 minute, 30 seconds
START CUE:	A kid opens his locker.
END TIME:	1 hour, 2 minutes, 45 seconds
END CUE:	The bully runs off.
DURATION:	1 minute, 15 seconds

Overview: A bully forces a kid to hand over his lunch money. Napoleon tells the kid to vote for Pedro—he offers protection. Later the bully tries to steal the kid's bike. But a low rider, with "Vote 4 Pedro" on the side, pulls up with Pedro's tough-looking cousins driving. The bully flees.

Illustration: Why don't we help people who are terrorized by bullies? Challenge your students to speak up for the rights of the "picked on" in their schools, showing the love of Christ by standing against the injustice roaming the halls.

Questions:
- What is the last thing you saw a bully do?
- Did you do anything to stop the bullying? Why or why not?
- Read 1 John 3:16-18. **What responsibility do we have in standing up against bullies?**
- What prevents a person from sticking up for the oppressed?
- How will standing up against bullies tangibly communicate the gospel?

Change | I CAN'T WEAR JEANS?

Title: **WHAT A GIRL WANTS**	
DRAMA Warner Brothers, 2003	PG

Scripture: Romans 12:1-2
Alternate Takes: Conformity (1 Thessalonians 5:4-8),
Family (Ruth 1:8-18)

DVD CHAPTER:	21
START TIME:	1 hour, 12 minutes, 45 seconds
START CUE:	Daphne reads a magazine on her bed.
END TIME:	1 hour, 14 minutes, 30 seconds
END CUE:	Henry exits.
DURATION:	1 minute, 45 seconds

Overview: Lord Dashwood shows Daphne portraits of her forefathers, explaining that the burden of their family is to follow certain codes of conduct. Daphne realizes she must change a little to fit in with the family.

Illustration: Change is never an easy thing, especially when you don't know whether you're supposed to accept it or not. Help your students discern the proper time to accept change and when to remain firm in their ways.

Questions:
- Do you think Daphne should change for the sake of the family? Why or why not?
- What is the most difficult change you've had to make?
- What positive things came from that change? What negative things?
- Read Romans 12:1-2. **What hints does this verse give for knowing when we should change?**
- What do you think God wants you to change in your life, and how will you go about doing that?

Character | WHAT ARE YOU BUILDING?

Title: THE EMPEROR'S CLUB	**PG-13**
DRAMA — Universal Pictures, 2002	

Scripture: Romans 5:1-5
Alternate Take: Influence (Matthew 5:13-16)

DVD CHAPTER:	3
START TIME:	8 minutes, 00 seconds
START CUE:	Martin walks to the back of the room.
END TIME:	10 minutes, 00 seconds
END CUE:	Hundert says, "Their story is our story."
DURATION:	2 minutes

Overview: Martin reads the details of Shutruk-Nahunte's exploits to the class. Mr. Hundert says conquest without contribution is without consequence—that's why history forgot this king. He points to historical giants whose character and contributions continue to impact the world today.

Illustration: Despite the scores of celebrities who seem to have everything—except morals—character does count. Pose Hundert's question to your own students, encouraging them to build the character that makes a positive contribution to God's kingdom.

Questions:
- What traits do you believe reflect true character?
- Are you cultivating this type of character in your own life? Why or why not?
- Read Romans 5:1-5. Why is good character so important in spiritual life?
- Without seeking to create trials, how can you build your character?

Choices | OPTION A OR OPTION B?

Title: THE RUNDOWN	**PG-13**
HUMOR — Universal Pictures, 2003	

Scripture: Joshua 24:14-15
Alternate Take: The Afterlife (Matthew 25:32-46)

DVD CHAPTER:	6
START TIME:	22 minutes, 15 seconds
START CUE:	Travis exits a bathroom.
END TIME:	23 minutes, 45 seconds
END CUE:	Beck says, "There is no option C."
DURATION:	1 minute, 30 seconds

Overview: Beck offers Travis two choices. Option A: Travis returns to Los Angeles with no trouble. Or option B: Travis returns to Los Angeles with broken bones. Travis picks option C and tries fighting Beck. He fails miserably.

Illustration: We have lots of choices in life, but it really boils down between serving God or serving everything else. Once we look at all our life decisions as A or B situations, it's much easier to make the right choice.

Questions:
- **What is the hardest thing for you about making choices?**
- Read Joshua 24:14-15. **How does every choice boil down to picking between God and something else?**
- **Is it possible to know with certainty which choice is the Christ-like one? Explain.**
- **What process can you use in any future choices that will help you include God and find his desire for your life?**

Christ-Likeness | PRACTICE MAKES PERFECT

DRAMA	Title: **MILLION DOLLAR BABY**	**PG-13**
	Warner Brothers, 2004	

Scripture: 1 John 3:1-10
Alternate Take: Spiritual Disciplines (1 Corinthians 9:24-27)

DVD CHAPTER:	10
START TIME:	36 minutes, 45 seconds
START CUE:	Maggie starts punching the speed bag.
END TIME:	39 minutes, 00 seconds
END CUE:	Frankie takes off his mitts.
DURATION:	2 minutes, 15 seconds

Overview: All day, every day, Maggie practices boxing at both the gym and every spare moment during her daily routine. She's getting stripped down to where she only hears her coach's voice, working so hard she will easily win her fight in the future.

Illustration: Becoming like Christ is a lot like training for boxing. It's a constant process that strips the person until all they hear is the voice of God's Spirit directing him or her. Discuss how your students can kick-start their training to become more Christ-like.

Questions:
- **What is the hardest training you've ever been through?**
- **Was it worth the hard work? Why or why not?**
- Read 1 John 3:1-10. **What statements in these verses surprise you?**
- **Do you think it's obvious that you're a child of God when people see you? Why or why not?**
- **What are some practical ways that you can train to become more Christ-like?**

A-C

Themes

DRAMA	**Title: ANTWONE FISHER**	**PG-13**
	Fox Searchlight, 2002	

Scripture: Acts 2:42-47

Alternate Takes: Community (Romans 12:10-13),
God's Family (Romans 12:4-5), Heaven (John 14:1-3)

DVD CHAPTER:	30
START TIME:	1 hour, 47 minutes, 45 seconds
START CUE:	Antwone approaches the front door.
END TIME:	1 hour, 50 minutes, 30 seconds
END CUE:	Everyone digs in and eats.
DURATION:	2 minutes, 45 seconds

Overview: Antwone enters the house and meets the huge extended family he never knew. They sit down and share a feast—one big happy family.

Illustration: What a heartwarming picture of what church should feel like! Discuss ways your church community can become a "house" full of love, acceptance, and community for all who enter.

Questions:
- **How is Antwone's experience in this clip similar to visiting our church? How is it different?**
- Read Acts 2:42-47. **Do you think church can be like this today? Why or why not?**
- **Why is it so important for churches to be friendly, welcoming places where people feel loved?**
- **What can we do to make our church and our ministry feel like the video clip and look like the early church?**

Cliques | WHERE DO I SIT?

HUMOR	**Title: MEAN GIRLS**	**PG-13**
	Paramount Pictures, 2004	

Scripture: Galatians 2:11-14

Alternate Take: Community (Romans 15:5-7)

DVD CHAPTER:	2
START TIME:	9 minutes, 00 seconds
START CUE:	Janis says, "Here. This map is going to be your guide."
END TIME:	9 minutes, 45 seconds
END CUE:	Janis says, "Beware of the Plastics."
DURATION:	45 seconds

Overview: Janis hands Cady a map of the cafeteria that lays out the school's social structure with all of the cliques clearly defined.

Illustration: Cliques seem a lot like death and taxes—they can't be avoided. Preach the radical notion of a world without cliques. It's a world God longs to see and asks us to create.

Questions:
- **What are the different cliques at your school?**
- **What problems do cliques create? what benefits?**
- Read Galatians 2:11-14. **Why did Paul get so hot about the clique the Jews were forming?**
- **How can cliques within the body of Christ hinder the growth of God's kingdom?**
- **How can we tear down any cliques that are forming within our church or ministry?**

Cloning | I'M THE ORIGINAL

HUMOR	Title: **THE SANTA CLAUSE 2**	
	Walt Disney Pictures, 2002	**G**

Scripture: Nehemiah 9:5-6

Alternate Take: Busyness (Luke 10:38-42)

DVD CHAPTER:	6
START TIME:	21 minutes, 45 seconds
START CUE:	Santa says, "I see where this is going."
END TIME:	24 minutes, 45 seconds
END CUE:	Toy Santa says, "Hello."
DURATION:	3 minutes

Overview: Curtis demonstrates how he can make a toy copy of Santa. That way, Santa can go see his family while the copy runs the North Pole. Santa agrees and goes through the machine, followed by a toy copy of himself.

Illustration: Is it morally acceptable to clone a person? How about an animal? What do you think about stem-cell research? Broach these topics with your youth because each medical advance will force them to confront these faith-shaking subjects.

Questions:
- **Would you clone yourself if you could? Why or why not?**
- **What are the ethical arguments against cloning? for cloning?**
- Read Nehemiah 9:5-6. **How would our gaining the ability to clone a human being affect God?**
- **What root beliefs and desires drive the push for human cloning?**
- **What is your personal stance on cloning in relation to your faith?**

Communication | EXCUSE ME?

HUMOR	**Title: ANGER MANAGEMENT**
	Columbia Pictures, 2003

PG-13

Scripture: Ephesians 4:17-27

Alternate Takes: Patriotism (Galatians 3:26-29), Racism (Esther 3:5-6)

DVD CHAPTER:	4
START TIME:	6 minutes, 15 seconds
START CUE:	Dave says, "Excuse me. Can I get a headset?"
END TIME:	8 minutes, 15 seconds
END CUE:	Buddy sleeps.
DURATION:	2 minutes, 00 seconds

Overview: Dave repeatedly requests a headset from the flight attendant. She warns him not to raise his voice (which he doesn't), and an air marshal steps in with accusations of racism. The marshal finally shocks Dave with a stun gun.

Illustration: How do we communicate God's timeless message (or any other truth, for that matter) with a world that either can't or refuses to hear it? Discuss some methods for clear communication so your youth don't receive any nasty "shocks" they might otherwise avoid.

Questions:
- Have you ever felt as if no one was listening to you or understanding you? What happened?
- What are some things that create barriers to clear communication?
- Read Ephesians 4:17-27. **What barriers exist between Christians and non-Christians when communicating God's truth?**
- Why are we supposed to continue trying to communicate God's love to these people no matter how difficult it might be?
- What are some practical ways you can bridge this communication gap?

Community | A LITTLE FRIENDLY HAZING

HUMOR	**Title: FINDING NEMO**
	Walt Disney Pictures, 2003

G

Scripture: Colossians 3:11-14

Alternate Take: Peer Pressure (Deuteronomy 13:6-8)

DVD CHAPTER:	12
START TIME:	36 minutes, 15 seconds
START CUE:	Nemo sleeps.
END TIME:	38 minutes, 45 seconds

A-C

Themes

END CUE:	They chant, "Shark bait, ooo, ba..."
DURATION:	2 minutes, 30 seconds

Overview: The fish stage an elaborate "rite of passage" for Nemo to become a part of their club. Nemo accepts their challenge to swim through the "ring of fire," and he's welcomed into the group.

Illustration: Deep down, everybody wants to be part of a group (which explains the rise in both gangs and Creative Memories groups). Tap into this primal urge, making your ministry a place where community grows naturally.

Questions:
- Why does everyone desire to be a part of some type of community?
- What needs do the groups you belong to fulfill?
- Read Colossians 3:11-14. What ingredients go into building a Christ-like community?
- What hurdles might prevent genuine community from happening within a body of believers?
- What must we do to make our ministry a stronger, more welcoming community?

Compassion | I NEVER LEARNED TO READ!

	Title: **HOLES**	**PG**
DRAMA	Walt Disney Pictures, 2003	

Scripture: James 1:27
Alternate Take: Rejection (Jeremiah 15:10-11)

DVD CHAPTER:	10
START TIME:	35 minutes, 45 seconds
START CUE:	Zero stands.
END TIME:	37 minutes, 00 seconds
END CUE:	Stanley exits.
DURATION:	1 minute, 15 seconds

Overview: Stanley tells Zero it's awkward having him read over his shoulder. Zero shrugs, "I can't read." He asks Stanley to teach him, but Stanley refuses because the long days of digging wear him out.

Illustration: Not many people would refuse a direct request like this, but we often turn away from the unspoken cries for help around us every day. We kill our compassion with busyness and excuses. Challenge your students to become compassionate, living out James' definition of pure religion that helps others.

Questions:
- Have you ever turned down someone who asked you for help? If so, why?
- Are Christians known for compassion? Explain.
- Read James 1:27. What excuses do people give for not following this command?

- How will becoming more compassionate bring people closer to God, both the helper and the person helped?
- What are some practical things you can do in your daily life to become more compassionate?

Complaining | I WANT SOMETHING BETTER

Title: **BARBERSHOP 2: BACK IN BUSINESS**	
HUMOR — MGM, 2004	PG-13

Scripture: Exodus 16:1-3
Alternate Take: Gratitude (Psalm 147:7-9)

DVD CHAPTER:	19
START TIME:	44 minutes, 15 seconds
START CUE:	Hamburger patties sizzle on the grill.
END TIME:	45 minutes, 00 seconds
END CUE:	Cal walks up.
DURATION:	45 seconds

Overview: Eddie gives a girl a hamburger, and she gripes that it's burnt. Eddie says it's free and to stop complaining. She refuses to eat it, so Eddie takes it back.

Illustration: It's amazing what some people gripe about. (Just the fact that Jesus forgives us our myriad of sins should make everything peachy!) Point out that we have nothing to complain about—ever—in the face of God's tremendous mercy and grace.

Questions:
- What is the dumbest thing you've ever heard someone complain about?
- Read Exodus 16:1-3. What would motivate Israel to complain a few days after God delivered them from slavery?
- When do you struggle most with the temptation to complain?
- How do our complaints reflect poorly upon God?
- How can you transform your complaints into praises for God?

Confession | I'VE GOT SOMETHING TO TELL YOU

Title: **JUST MARRIED**	
HUMOR — 20th Century Fox, 2003	PG-13

Scripture: 1 John 1:6-10
Alternate Takes: Honesty (Psalm 15), Lies (Proverbs 19:9)

DVD CHAPTER:	19
START TIME:	1 hour, 1 minute, 00 seconds
START CUE:	Tom enters.

END TIME:	1 hour, 3 minutes, 15 seconds
END CUE:	Sara says, "It was more like a lie."
DURATION:	2 minutes, 15 seconds

Overview: Sara asks Tom if he's always told her the truth or if he let a lie go so long that it got too big for him to come clean. Tom admits her dog didn't die from chasing a pigeon, but because he accidentally threw a ball out the window.

Warning: *Sara uses a curse word after the clip ends at 1:03:20.*

Illustration: It's never fun to admit you've done something wrong (especially when it caused a pet's death). But God calls us to confess regularly, so help your young people learn this important practice.

Questions:
- **What is the worst thing you've ever had to confess to someone? What happened?**
- **What makes confessing our mistakes so hard, even to our closest friends?**
- Read 1 John 1:6-10. **Do you think this is a little harsh? Why or why not?**
- **How might regular confession improve your personal relationships? your relationship with God?**
- **What can you do to make confession a natural, normal part of your routine?**

Conflict | YOU'RE A STUPID DOO DOO HEAD

	Title: **HOOK**	
HUMOR	TriStar Pictures, 1991	**PG**

Scripture: Luke 12:58-59
Alternate Takes: Put-Downs (Ephesians 4:29),
Taming the Tongue (Proverbs 10:18-21)

DVD CHAPTER:	15
START TIME:	1 hour, 14 minutes, 00 seconds
START CUE:	Peter asks, "Eat what?"
END TIME:	1 hour, 16 minutes, 00 seconds
END CUE:	Peter sits.
DURATION:	2 minutes, 00 seconds

Overview: Peter and Rufio get into an absurd name-calling contest, going back and forth tearing each other down until Rufio doesn't have a comeback.

Illustration: Everyone experiences conflict in life. But how we respond to it separates the adults from the lost little boys. Give your teens some practical, Bible-based tools for dealing with the conflicts that come their way.

Questions:
- **What are some ways you've seen people deal with conflict, besides just name-calling?**
- **How do you typically respond to conflict? Does it work? Explain.**

- Read Luke 12:58-59. **According to these verses, what is Jesus' approach toward conflict?**
- **Is Jesus saying we should simply lie down every time we experience conflict? Explain.**
- **How do you need to change your approach toward conflict in the future so it mirrors Jesus' heart?**

Conformity | I WANNA BE A CLONE

Title: STAR WARS EPISODE II: ATTACK OF THE CLONES	PG
DRAMA 20th Century Fox, 2002	

Scripture: Romans 12:1-8
Alternate Take: Cloning (Job 14:1-5)

DVD CHAPTER:	20
START TIME:	45 minutes, 45 seconds
START CUE:	A huge room filled with clones is shown on the screen.
END TIME:	47 minutes, 00 seconds
END CUE:	The Prime Minister says, "We keep him here."
DURATION:	1 minute, 15 seconds

Overview: The Kaminoan Prime Minister takes Obi-Wan on a tour of the clone army—thousands of exact replicas of bounty hunter Jango Fett.

Illustration: *Conformity* is almost a dirty word these days, even though the masses subconsciously strive for it. The Bible warns against becoming unduly influenced by "the world." On the flip side, God's children should not become carbon copies of their Christian brothers and sisters either. God created each person uniquely and wonderfully, not in bulk.

Questions:
- **How does the media try to get people to conform? How does your school? your friends? the church?**
- **What are the positives to conforming? What are the negatives?**
- Read Romans 12:1-8. **What, in your own words, does "transformed by the renewing of your mind" mean, and how does someone do that?**
- **Does "conforming" to Christ bring people freedom or make them clones? Explain.**

Contentment | I WANT A DIFFERENT LIFE

HUMOR	Title: **SHARK TALE**	PG
	DreamWorks, 2004	

Scripture: Phillipians 4:10-13
Alternate Take: Self-Worth (Galatians 6:3-5)

DVD CHAPTER:	6
START TIME:	15 minutes, 00 seconds
START CUE:	A close-up of Oscar's black eye is shown on the screen.
END TIME:	16 minutes, 45 seconds
END CUE:	Angie says, "You don't have to live at the top of the reef to be a somebody."
DURATION:	1 minute, 45 seconds

Overview: Oscar longs to be somebody rich and famous, living at the top of the reef. He remembers idolizing his dad working at the wash—until he realized no one respects scrubbers. Angie tells Oscar he doesn't need to live at the top to be somebody.

Illustration: We sure have a lot of discontented people running around in the richest nation in history. Help your young people draw contentment not only from their extreme wealth (on the world scale) but especially from their relationship with Jesus Christ as Lord and Savior.

Questions:
- Can you relate to Oscar? Why or why not?
- Read Philippians 4:10-13. Are you content in every situation? Why or why not?
- What are we really saying to God when we are discontent?
- What attitudes or beliefs can you hold on to that will help you remain content?
- How can you fight any discontentment you are experiencing at the moment?

Courage | I DON'T LOOK AT ODDS

DRAMA	Title: **THE SCORPION KING**	PG-13
	Universal Pictures, 2002	

Scripture: 1 Samuel 14:1-14
Alternate Take: God's Power (Psalm 68:32-35)

DVD CHAPTER:	11
START TIME:	40 minutes, 15 seconds
START CUE:	Mathayus rides a camel.
END TIME:	41 minutes, 15 seconds
END CUE:	The sandstorm hits.
DURATION:	1 minute

Overview: Mathayus attacks Memnon's men—one on 12. They think he's crazy, until a massive sandstorm rolls in behind him.

Illustration: God can grant his children unlimited courage, even when facing insurmountable odds. Help your students tap into this reservoir of courage so they can fearlessly face any challenge.

Questions:
- How would you define *courage*?
- What is the most courageous thing you have ever done?
- Read 1 Samuel 14:1-14. Do you think Jonathan was courageous or foolish? Explain.
- What prevents you from showing more courage in both your physical and spiritual life?
- What must you do in order to receive the courage that God offers his followers?

Curiosity | I JUST WANT TO PEEK

Title: THE LORD OF THE RINGS: THE RETURN OF THE KING		PG-13
DRAMA	New Line Cinema, 2003	

Scripture: 1 Samuel 6:13-19

Alternate Takes: Disobedience (Nehemiah 9:24-31), The Occult (Leviticus 19:31), Sin (James 1:13-15)

DVD CHAPTER:	6
START TIME:	19 minutes, 45 seconds
START CUE:	Pippin wakes up.
END TIME:	22 minutes, 00 seconds
END CUE:	Pippin says, "Forgive me."
DURATION:	2 minutes, 15 seconds

Overview: Pippin takes the palantir from Gandalf while he sleeps—even though he knows he shouldn't. The ball summons the Dark Lord, Sauron, whose probing eye tortures the hobbit until Aragorn and Gandalf come to his rescue.

Illustration: Curiosity has been known to kill more than cats. Help your young people learn to discern the difference between appropriate and potentially hazardous curiosity so they don't make any painful mistakes.

Questions:
- Have you ever been burned by your curiosity? If so, what happened?
- Read 1 Samuel 6:13-19. Do you think the punishment for looking in the ark was fair? Why or why not?
- What are some potentially dangerous things that have piqued your curiosity?
- How does a person discern when to pursue curiosity and when to turn away?
- How can you protect yourself from succumbing to inappropriate curiosity?

Dancing | DISCO INFERNO

HUMOR

Title: **NAPOLEON DYNAMITE**

Fox Searchlight, 2004

PG

Scripture: Psalm 149:1-5

Alternate Takes: Confidence (Romans 8:28-31),
Creativity (Exodus 31:1-5)

DVD CHAPTER:	18
START TIME:	1 hour, 20 minutes, 15 seconds
START CUE:	Napoleon walks on stage.
END TIME:	1 hour, 23 minutes, 00 seconds
END CUE:	Everyone gets to their feet.
DURATION:	2 minutes, 45 seconds

Overview: Napoleon performs an elaborate interpretive dance for the entire school. He runs off stage, and the audience goes nuts with applause.

Illustration: There's a wide spectrum of dancing—from the kind that glorifies God to the kind on MTV. Help your students find the line between a dance fever that pleases their Lord and what incites the fires of lust.

Questions:
- **What are some reasons people have for dancing?**
- Read Psalm 149:1-5. **Have you ever seen someone praise God through dance? If so, how is it different from other types of dancing?**
- **Why do some Christians claim that dancing is a sin?**
- **Where is the line between dancing that glorifies God and all other types of dance?**

Death | WHAT WILL THEY SAY?

DRAMA

Title: **BIG FISH**

Columbia Pictures, 2003

PG-13

Scripture: Philippians 3:7-14

Alternate Takes: Heaven (Philippians 3:18-21),
Inheritance (Hebrews 11:1-13)

DVD CHAPTER:	27
START TIME:	1 hour, 53 minutes, 00 seconds
START CUE:	Will carries Ed.
END TIME:	1 hour, 56 minutes, 00 seconds
END CUE:	Ed says, "Exactly."
DURATION:	3 minutes

Overview: Will carries Ed down to the river through a crowd of people he knew throughout his life. He takes his dying father out into the river and releases him, allowing him to die.

Illustration: Not to be creepy, but encourage the kids to examine death. We know it's the ultimate goal line, so how will they play the game in the meantime? By living in excellence now, they will assure themselves a glorious reward when they leave this earth.

Questions:
- What kind of legacy do you hope to leave when you die?
- Read Philippians 3:7-14. **How does following Paul's advice in these verses prepare a person for death?**
- How can living a good life make death a joyful event?
- What must you start doing in order to fashion a life that warrants an honorable death?

Dedication | I'M LIKE CLOCKWORK

	Title: **SUPER SIZE ME**	
HUMOR	Samuel Goldwyn Films, 2004	PG

Scripture: Joshua 22:5
Alternate Take: Stagnation (Isaiah 43:18-19)

DVD CHAPTER:	16
START TIME:	42 minutes, 00 seconds
START CUE:	A McDonald's clerk asks, "How many?"
END TIME:	43 minutes, 45 seconds
END CUE:	"Party With Big Mac."
DURATION:	1 minute, 45 seconds

Overview: Don Gorske explains his love for the Big Mac and how he's had at least two a day every day for years. He then bites into the 19,000th Big Mac of his life.

Illustration: If we could only dedicate ourselves to Christ with the same vigor Don Gorske dedicates himself to Big Mac hamburgers, the world would transform in the blink of an eye. Challenge your youth to examine their level of spiritual dedication and to up the ante if necessary.

Questions:
- What do you think of Don's dedication to the Big Mac?
- What are some things you are dedicated to, and why do you like them?
- Read Joshua 22:5. **What does this level of dedication look like in everyday life?**
- Why don't we see many Christians strive for this high level of dedication to their Lord and Savior?
- How can you dedicate yourself more wholeheartedly to God?

Denying Christ | ARE YOU ASHAMED OF ME?

HUMOR

Title: **STUCK ON YOU**

20th Century Fox, 2003

PG-13

Scripture: Matthew 10:32-33
Alternate Take: Shame (Psalm 25:1-5)

DVD CHAPTER:	8
START TIME:	37 minutes, 15 seconds
START CUE:	The brothers sit on the bed.
END TIME:	38 minutes, 15 seconds
END CUE:	A knock sounds at the door.
DURATION:	1 minute

Overview: Bob confesses he didn't tell Mae about Walt, his conjoined twin. He even cut Walt out of the pictures he sent her. Walk thinks Bob is ashamed of him.

Illustration: It's a terrible thing to cut Jesus out of your pictures. Make sure your teens understand the seriousness of denying our Lord before others.

Questions:
- Why might someone be ashamed of a relationship with Jesus, cutting him out of the picture?
- Have you ever done this to Jesus? If so, why?
- Read Matthew 10:32-33. **Does this mean a person who denies Jesus can never have eternal life? Why or why not?**
- What common everyday situations might tempt you to deny Jesus?
- How can you learn to stand boldly for Christ at all times, refusing to ever deny him?

Discipleship | ARE YOU IN OR OUT?

DRAMA

Title: **ARMAGEDDON**

Touchstone Pictures, 1998

PG-13

Scripture: Luke 14:25-33
Alternate Take: Sacrifice (Luke 9:23-24)

DVD CHAPTER:	5
START TIME:	32 minutes, 15 seconds
START CUE:	Everyone sits at a coffee table.
END TIME:	33 minutes, 30 seconds
END CUE:	Rockhound says, "You think we'll get hazard pay out of this?"
DURATION:	1 minute, 15 seconds

Overview: Stamper asks his team members if they'll join him in saving the world. All of them agree to risk their lives and join him.

Illustration: Jesus' call to join him isn't a tossed off "Want to come along for the ride?" query. He demands a lot of his disciples, and your young people should be clear on his requirements before agreeing to walk in his footsteps.

Questions:
- Do you think the men in this scene have truly thought through their decision? Why or why not?
- Read Luke 14:25-33. What is the true cost of becoming a disciple of Jesus Christ?
- Why doesn't Jesus make it easy to follow him?
- Are you willing to pay the price Jesus demands of his disciples? Explain.

Discipline | YOU'VE BEEN A BAD BOY

DRAMA	Title: **COACH CARTER**	PG-13
	Paramount Pictures, 2005	

Scripture: Hebrews 12:5-11
Alternate Takes: Forgiveness (Matthew 18:21-22), Mercy (Matthew 5:7)

DVD CHAPTER:	10
START TIME:	56 minutes, 45 seconds
START CUE:	Mrs. Battle enters the store.
END TIME:	59 minutes, 45 seconds
END CUE:	Mrs. Battle and Junior exit.
DURATION:	3 minutes

Overview: Mrs. Battle knows her son broke the rules and shouldn't receive special treatment, but she still asks Carter to consider letting him play. Coach says he needs to hear it from Junior, and she drags him inside. Junior apologizes and promises to fulfill his obligations. Coach gives him a stiff punishment but allows him back on the team.

Illustration: Though never fun to receive, God metes out discipline in love. Teach your students to accept his discipline with the same joy Junior displays, seeing the glorious big picture rather than the momentary discomfort.

Questions:
- Have you ever been appreciative of discipline? If so, why?
- Read Hebrews 12:5-11. How is discipline a sign of love?
- Why can't God teach us righteousness without discipline?
- The next time you're disciplined, how can you keep your eyes focused on the big picture rather than the temporary discomfort?

Dishonesty | BLACK IS WHITE

HUMOR	Title: **INTOLERABLE CRUELTY**	**PG-13**
	Universal Pictures, 2003	

Scripture: Psalm 101:5-8
Alternate Take: Truth (Zechariah 8:16-17)

DVD CHAPTER:	2
START TIME:	10 minutes, 00 seconds
START CUE:	Miles stares at his client.
END TIME:	12 minutes, 00 seconds
END CUE:	Miles closes the door.
DURATION:	2 minutes

Overview: Miles questions his client, twisting her infidelity into an obviously fabricated story about her being the true victim. She can't believe Miles could actually sell people his slant, but he's confident in his ability to convince the jury of the "truth."

Illustration: God hates dishonesty, yet our society seems to honor those who can shade and twist the truth to fit their purposes. Expose these deceptions for what they are—sin.

Questions:
- Why does our society honor people who can twist the truth this way?
- What are some other ways people use dishonesty in everyday life?
- Read Psalm 101:5-8. Why does God hate dishonesty so much?
- When are you the most tempted to be dishonest?
- How will you build the strength to withstand those temptations?

Disobedience | I'LL DO IT MY WAY

HUMOR	Title: **THE CAT IN THE HAT**	**PG**
	Universal Pictures, 2003	

Scripture: Leviticus 10:1-3
Alternate Take: Discipline (Proverbs 29:15)

DVD CHAPTER:	3
START TIME:	6 minutes, 00 seconds
START CUE:	Conrad says, "Ladies and gentlemen."
END TIME:	8 minutes, 00 seconds
END CUE:	Mom finishes, "...the exact opposite of what I say."
DURATION:	2 minutes

Overview: Conrad pads himself with loaves of bread and rides a pan like a sled down the stairs despite his sister's warnings. Mom witnesses Conrad making a huge mess and grounds him on the spot for his disobedience.

Illustration: It doesn't matter how many times and how many ways God says, no, we still refuse to obey all of his commands. Help your young people curb their more rebellious inclinations, squeezing disobedience out of their immoral fiber.

Questions:
- **When was the last time you directly disobeyed your parents? What happened?**
- **Why did you disobey them?**
- Read Leviticus 10:1-3. **What motivated the sons' disobedience?**
- **Why does God react so harshly against the disobedient?**
- **How can you learn to become obedient to God in the areas where you struggle with obedience?**

Doubt | ARE YOU SURE?

| DRAMA | Title: **THE LORD OF THE RINGS: THE RETURN OF THE KING** | PG-13 |
| | New Line Cinema, 2003 | |

Scripture: Psalm 77:11-20

Alternate Takes: Deceit (Leviticus 19:11), Distrust (Psalm 118:6-9)

DVD CHAPTER:	17
START TIME:	57 minutes, 30 seconds
START CUE:	Gollum says, "Master carries heavy burden."
END TIME:	58 minutes, 00 seconds
END CUE:	Frodo clutches the ring to his chest.
DURATION:	30 seconds

Overview: With Sam out of earshot, Gollum laces Frodo's mind with doubt, insinuating that Sam's true goal is to gain the One Ring for himself. Frodo takes these (obviously treacherous) words to heart, immediately doubting his friend's loyalty.

Illustration: Gollum mirrors the devil, whispering lies to faithful followers of Christ. Doubt in itself is not sin, but might lead to a spiritual disconnect, rejecting God's truth if unchecked. Make your ministry a safe place for expressing uncertainty and finding answers, reminding each "doubting Thomas" he or she can take it straight to God.

Questions:
- **How are Gollum's actions similar to what the devil does to Christians concerning faith issues?**
- **Is it a sin to doubt? Explain.**
- Read Psalm 77:11-20. **How can you apply these verses to resolving any doubts you have?**
- **Why are Christians typically reluctant to share their doubts?**
- **How can we make this ministry a safe place to honestly discuss our doubts?**

Dreams | WHEN I GROW UP...

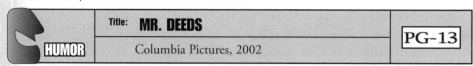

HUMOR

Title: **MR. DEEDS**

Columbia Pictures, 2002

PG-13

Scripture: Psalm 37:4-6

Alternate Takes: Greed (1 Timothy 6:9-11), Legacy (Proverbs 22:1)

DVD CHAPTER:	26
START TIME:	1 hour, 20 minutes, 45 seconds
START CUE:	Deeds says, "Hello, everybody."
END TIME:	1 hour, 22 minutes, 00 seconds
END CUE:	The cowboy sits.
DURATION:	1 minute, 15 seconds

Overview: Deeds believes being rich and powerful isn't bad, but doing anything for money is. Kids always dream of helping people. Deeds asks a room of wealthy people what they dreamed of doing. They admit wanting to be vets, senators, and so forth.

Illustration: Discuss your students' dreams, helping them funnel those visions of fame and fortune into a desire to build God's kingdom, trusting that God will bring their desires to fruition in ways that please and glorify him.

Questions:
- What do you dream of doing?
- What are you doing to make that dream come true?
- Read Psalm 37:4-6. **How does your dream fit within your relationship with God?**
- **Why don't all of the desires of our hearts come true if God promises to bring them forth?**
- **How can you prevent your dream from distracting you from your devotion to God?**

Drunkenness | I'M JUST GETTING STARTED

HUMOR

Title: **THE SPONGEBOB SQUAREPANTS MOVIE**

Paramount Pictures, 2004

PG

Scripture: Proverbs 20:1

Alternate Take: Gluttony (Proverbs 23:19-21)

DVD CHAPTER:	3
START TIME:	16 minutes, 30 seconds
START CUE:	SpongeBob cries at the nut bar.
END TIME:	18 minutes, 45 seconds
END CUE:	SpongeBob and Patrick pass out on stage.
DURATION:	2 minutes, 15 seconds

Overview: SpongeBob tries to drown his depression over not receiving a promotion by eating humongous sundaes with Patrick. The friends eat round after round of sundaes until they're acting crazy drunk.

Illustration: It crosses all cultures, creeds, and classes—drunk people look like idiots. No one glorifies God when drunk, so slap some sense into your students before they pull a "SpongeBob."

Questions:
- What's the dumbest thing you've ever seen a drunk person do?
- Why do people choose to get drunk even though it always makes them look stupid?
- Read Proverbs 20:1. **Can a drunk person ever glorify God? Why or why not?**
- How does drunkenness damage a person's social reputation? his or her relationship with God?
- What safeguards can you set up to prevent yourself from becoming drunk?

Duty | NOTHING'S GONNA STAND IN MY WAY

Title: **MASTER AND COMMANDER:** THE FAR SIDE OF THE WORLD		PG-13
DRAMA	20th Century Fox, 2003	

Scripture: Matthew 5:13-16

Alternate Takes: Accountability (Proverbs 27:17), Pride (Proverbs 8:13)

DVD CHAPTER:	16
START TIME:	55 minutes, 30 seconds
START CUE:	A man begins to enter with a light.
END TIME:	57 minutes, 00 seconds
END CUE:	Stephen finishes, "... nothing personal in this call to duty?"
DURATION:	1 minute, 30 seconds

Overview: Stephen calls into question Jack's actions, asking if he might possibly be giving into personal pride and placing the crew at risk with his orders. Jack insists it's his duty to fight the French, and he's determined to fulfill that duty, no matter the cost to himself and his crew.

Illustration: What exactly is our "duty" as Christians? Help your young people distinguish exactly what they should hold up as duties toward God, family, and country. Encourage them to stick with their duties no matter what the circumstances, living with an integrity that glorifies God.

Questions:
- What are some duties every person has to his or her family? country? God?
- Do you think people take duty seriously today? Explain.
- Read Matthew 5:13-16. **Do you think Christians in general are doing a good job of fulfilling the duty in these verses? Are you? Explain.**
- What are some practical ways a person can spread "salt" and "light"?
- How can you fulfill your Christian duties this week?

Easter | HE'S ALIVE!

Title: **PETER PAN**	**PG**
DRAMA	Universal Pictures, 2003	

Scripture: Matthew 28:1-10

Alternate Takes: Belief (Matthew 21:21-22), Elijah (1 Kings 17:17-24), Lazarus (John 11:32-44)

DVD CHAPTER:	19
START TIME:	1 hour, 15 minutes, 00 seconds
START CUE:	Peter's face next to the dead Tinker Bell.
END TIME:	1 hour, 17 minutes, 45 seconds
END CUE:	Hook shouts, "He's alive!"
DURATION:	2 minutes, 45 seconds

Overview: Peter, Wendy, and the boys start chanting, "I do believe in fairies!" As their chant grows, Tinker Bell comes back to life, the snow stops falling, and spring bursts forth.

Illustration: And on the third day, he rose from the dead. Use this scene to communicate the rapturous joy of the disciples on that history-shaking day when Jesus Christ conquered the grave.

Questions:
- What emotions must have run through the disciples when they heard Jesus was alive?
- What do you think your response will be when you see Jesus in the flesh for the first time?
- Read Matthew 28:1-10. How does this historical event separate Christianity from every other religion?
- Why does the Christian faith hinge on the death and resurrection of Jesus?

Encouragement | YOU'RE REALLY GREAT!

Title: **CATCH ME IF YOU CAN**	**PG-13**
DRAMA	DreamWorks, 2002	

Scripture: Isaiah 35:3-4

Alternate Take: Comfort (2 Corinthians 1:3-7)

DVD CHAPTER:	13
START TIME:	1 hour, 11 minutes, 00 seconds
START CUE:	Frank walks down the hospital hall.
END TIME:	1 hour, 13 minutes, 00 seconds
END CUE:	Brenda says, "Thank you."
DURATION:	2 minutes

Overview: Frank witnesses Brenda, a hospital candy striper, get reamed by a doctor. Frank cheers her up by commending her work. Brenda doesn't believe him. Frank then reveals he hated having braces, but she looks good in them. Brenda brightens considerably with his encouragement.

Illustration: It's amazing that such a powerful salve to the wounds of society—simple words of affirmation and encouragement—is used so sparingly. Christians have the opportunity and moral duty to uplift those around them with smiles, hugs, and positive words. Challenge your young people to open the floodgates of goodwill by simply recognizing opportunities to build people up.

Questions:
- Why do simple compliments and common kindness mean so much to people?
- If encouragement is such a great thing, why don't people—yourself included—do it more often?
- Read Isaiah 35:3-4. **What benefits come from encouraging others, to both the giver and the receiver?**
- How would the world change if we encouraged one another more?
- What can you do to make encouragement a part of your daily life?

Equality | YOUR ROOM IS READY

HUMOR	**Title: DIE ANOTHER DAY** MGM, 2002	**PG-13**

Scripture: James 2:1-4

Alternate Takes: Heaven (2 Corinthians 5:1-3)

DVD CHAPTER:	8
START TIME:	27 minutes, 15 seconds
START CUE:	Bond climbs on the dock.
END TIME:	28 minutes, 30 seconds
END CUE:	Bond says, "Just surviving."
DURATION:	1 minute, 15 seconds

Overview: A bedraggled, sopping wet Bond strides into a posh hotel clad in hospital pajamas. While the snooty guests turn up their collective noses at his unkempt state, the hotel's maitre d' immediately offers him a suite, treating him as an honored guest despite his outrageous appearance.

Illustration: This scene perfectly depicts the example of equality given by James, the brother of Jesus. Human (or sin) nature provides deferential treatment to the wealthy, beautiful, famous, and powerful. Not in God's kingdom, where every table is round. Explore equality, seeing people free of judgment.

Questions:
- What reasons do people have for not always treating others as equals?
- How does this inequality affect society? you personally?

- Read James 2:1-4. **Why does God want us to treat everyone as equal, even people who hate him?**
- **How can a person come to a place where they see all people with equality?**
- **What types of people do you struggle with seeing as equal to yourself, and how can you change this attitude?**

Ethics | WHERE'S THE LINE AGAIN?

DRAMA	Title: **THE RAINMAKER**	PG-13
	Paramount Pictures, 1997	

Scripture: Romans 1:18-25
Alternate Take: Integrity (2 Corinthians 4:1-2)

DVD CHAPTER:	32
START TIME:	2 hours, 7 minutes, 45 seconds
START CUE:	Shifflet puts on his hat.
END TIME:	2 hours, 9 minutes, 00 seconds
END CUE:	Closing credits begin.
DURATION:	1 minute, 15 seconds

Overview: Rudy and Shifflet say goodbye. Rudy could continue scoring big settlements if he didn't care what methods he used to get them. He realizes that lawyers make constant choices about crossing the line, and eventually that line disappears.

Illustration: It's important to instill a strong sense of biblical ethics within our young people because the moral line is constantly being assaulted. Hopefully, by drawing a line in the wet concrete now, it won't disappear once they enter college or the work-place.

Questions:
- **How would you define your "ethics"?**
- **Are ethics the same for all people? Why or why not?**
- Read Romans 1:18-25. **How does a Christian discern the proper ethics to live by?**
- **Why is there a diversity of opinion among Christians concerning proper ethics if God has placed them inside our hearts?**
- **How can you strengthen your ethics so you can overcome the temptation to cross over the line?**

Euthanasia | DON'T DO IT

DRAMA	Title: **MILLION DOLLAR BABY**	PG-13
	Warner Brothers, 2004	

Scripture: Deuteronomy 32:39
Alternate Takes: Compassion (Colossians 3:12),
Counsel (Proverbs 11:14)

DVD CHAPTER:	33
START TIME:	1 hour, 56 minutes, 15 seconds
START CUE:	Frankie sits in church with his priest.
END TIME:	1 hour, 58 minutes, 30 seconds
END CUE:	The priest leaves Frankie alone.
DURATION:	2 minutes, 15 seconds

Overview: Frankie tells his priest he can't help Maggie die. It's a horrible sin, but he's convinced keeping her alive is killing her also. The priest claims doing such a thing leads to a place he can never return from. A tormented Frankie weeps over his dilemma.

Illustration: More and more will experience this dilemma as medical science continues to prolong life and society keeps chipping away at the sanctity of life. That's why it's important to discuss euthanasia. Help your teens find the truth within this thorny issue so they will know the right thing to do in this terrible situation.

Questions:
- **What arguments have you heard for and against euthanasia?**
- **What is your personal opinion on the matter?**
- Read Deuteronomy 32:39. **How does this verse address the issue of euthanasia?**
- **How does euthanasia disrespect God?**
- **What areas might euthanasia move into if we allow it for the elderly or disabled?**

Evangelism | THE BEACH IS COVERED

Title: **WHALE RIDER**	
DRAMA	Newmarket Films, 2002

PG–13

Scripture: Matthew 9:35-38
Alternate Takes: Animals (Psalm 8), Non-Christians (John 3:16-21)

DVD CHAPTER:	21
START TIME:	1 hour, 17 minutes, 45 seconds
START CUE	Pai looks out the window.
END TIME:	1 hour, 19 minutes, 15 seconds
END CUE:	People hug.
DURATION:	1 minute, 30 seconds

Overview: Dying whales cover the beach. People work desperately to keep the whales alive, hoping to rescue them.

Illustration: What a powerful picture of the desperate need for workers in the spiritual harvest God has prepared! Use this scene to open the teenagers' eyes to the need and kick off a discussion for practical ways to save those dying on the beach.

Questions:
- **Why are these people even bothering to try and help in what's obviously a hopeless situation?**

- Read Matthew 9:35-38. **What in your opinion is the most discouraging or intimidating aspect of evangelism?**
- **What reasons do we have for ignoring the people dying spiritually around us?**
- **How can you overcome these fears and hurdles to evangelism?**
- **What are some simple, practical ways that you can share the lifesaving message of Jesus Christ with those around you?**

Evidence | I'M NOT CONVINCED

HUMOR	Title: **ELF**	PG
	New Line Cinema, 2003	

Scripture: Matthew 16:1-4
Alternate Take: Belief (John 20:24-31)

DVD CHAPTER:	15
START TIME:	1 hour, 19 minutes, 45 seconds
START CUE:	Walter says, "So you're uh..."
END TIME:	1 hour, 21 minutes, 30 seconds
END CUE:	Santa Claus says, "The paparazzi have been tryin' to nail me for years."
DURATION:	1 minute, 45 seconds

Overview: Buddy, Walter, and Michael help Santa fix his sleigh. Santa proves his credentials by giving Michael the exact skateboard he wants. The sleigh rises off the ground momentarily, powered by Christmas spirit. Michael wants to get the TV cameras because then everyone will believe, but Santa wants belief without sight.

Illustration: Do you ever wish Jesus would do that—show up at halftime of the Super Bowl and prove his existence? Help your ministry find the evidence that's out there concerning Jesus' existence and redemptive work on the cross.

Questions:
- **Do you think people would turn to Jesus if they had definitive evidence of his resurrection? Why or why not?**
- Read Matthew 16:1-4. **Why did Jesus refuse the Pharisees and Sadducees' request?**
- **What evidence do you cling to concerning Jesus' claims?**
- **What are some ways you can build in faith upon this evidence?**

Expectations | THIS ISN'T WHAT I IMAGINED

HUMOR	Title: **SHREK 2**	PG
	DreamWorks, 2004	

Scripture: Exodus 2:11-14
Alternate Take: Pride (Proverbs 29:23)

DVD CHAPTER:	1
START TIME:	45 seconds
START CUE:	A leather-bound book lies on a table.
END TIME:	2 minutes, 30 seconds
END CUE:	Prince Charming says, "With whom?"
DURATION:	1 minute, 45 seconds

Overview: Prince Charming recounts the tale of Princess Fiona and how only his kiss can break the spell that transforms her into an ogre each night. Unexpectedly, he finds a wolf lying in Fiona's bed and the princess off on her honeymoon.

Illustration: Our expectations sure give God a good laugh. Whenever we think we've got everything figured out, things fall apart. Help your youth find that solid ground of faith to stand on whenever the unexpected blindsides them.

Questions:

- **When was the last time that your expectations weren't met? What happened?**
- **Do you find it difficult to deal with unmet expectations? Why or why not?**
- Read aloud Exodus 2:11-14. **How did Moses probably expect the Israelites to respond to his actions?**
- **How did God use the unexpected to bring about a great miracle through Moses?**
- **What can you learn from Moses' experience that will help you deal with unmet expectations in the future?**

Facades | SURE I DROVE NASCAR

HUMOR	**Title: GUESS WHO**	**PG-13**
	Columbia Pictures, 2005	

Scripture: Genesis 20:1-13
Alternate Takes: Lies (Job 27:2-4), Pressure (Psalm 94:19)

DVD CHAPTER:	5
START TIME:	17 minutes, 15 seconds
START CUE:	Percy says, "Simon, you play any sports?"
END TIME:	19 minutes, 30 seconds
END CUE:	Simon says, "I shoulda went with hockey."
DURATION:	2 minutes, 15 seconds

Overview: Percy asks Simon if he plays sports—because you can't be a real man if you don't. Simon suddenly claims he was in Jeff Gordon's pit crew until a nasty wreck got it out of his system. Later Theresa confronts Simon on his obvious lie. Simon justifies the ruse because Percy intimidated him.

Illustration: There are hundreds of reasons for putting on a facade but one fantastic one for taking it off is God's command for his people to be authentic. Tear off any facades that are lurking within your group, helping each young person live with confidence in the personality that God gave him or her.

Questions:

- What are some different facades that you've seen people put up? that you've put up?
- Do facades have positive results? Why or why not?
- Read Genesis 20:1-13. Was Abraham justified in putting up his facade?
- How might honesty from the outset have served Abraham better?
- When are you most tempted to put up a facade, and how will you overcome that temptation?

Faith | IT CAN TAKE IT

DRAMA	Title: **K-19: THE WIDOWMAKER** Paramount Pictures, 2002	PG-13

Scripture: 1 Peter 1:3-9
Alternate Take: Risk (Matthew 14:25-31)

DVD CHAPTER:	5
START TIME:	37 minutes, 15 seconds
START CUE:	Vostrikov enters the bridge.
END TIME:	40 minutes, 15 seconds
END CUE:	The sub levels.
DURATION:	3 minutes

Overview: Vostrikov orders the sub to make a steep dive. With the increased depth, the crew grows more nervous. Vostrikov pushes them to 300 meters—the threshold of "crush depth." The sub's hull struggles under the pressure but holds.

Illustration: How deep can your faith go? Discuss ways to increase the strength of your faith so you can stand with confidence under even the most intense pressure.

Questions:

- Do you feel as if your faith in God can withstand a lot of pressure? Why or why not?
- Read 1 Peter 1:3-9. Why does our faith have to be tested?
- Where has God been testing your faith?
- How can you work to build the strength of your faith so it will survive the "depths" of any trial?

Faith Sharing | IT'S HARD TO EXPLAIN

HUMOR	Title: **NATIONAL TREASURE** Walt Disney Pictures, 2004	PG

Scripture: Acts 22:1-24
Alternate Takes: Faith (John 20:24-31), God's Ways (Isaiah 55:8-9)

DVD CHAPTER:	3
START TIME:	24 minutes, 00 seconds
START CUE:	Abigail says, "You told my assistant..."
END TIME:	26 minutes, 30 seconds
END CUE:	Abigail says, "Nice to meet you, too."
DURATION:	2 minutes, 30 seconds

Overview: Ben and Riley claim that the Declaration of Independence will be stolen. Abigail assures them it's impossible, but they proceed to tell her about the invisible treasure map on the back. Abigail obviously thinks they're nuts as their story, though true, grows ever more incredible.

Illustration: Ever feel this way when trying to explain the gospel to someone? Thankfully, the Holy Spirit can make what's clouded clear to even the hardest heart. Encourage your youth to seek his help and guidance when explaining their faith to others.

Questions:

- **Do you feel like this when trying to explain your faith in Jesus to someone? Why or why not?**
- **What is the hardest thing for you to explain to other people about your faith?**
- Read Acts 22:1-24. **How does the response to Paul's testimony make you feel about sharing your faith?**
- **What is our responsibility when it comes to sharing our faith? What isn't?**
- **How can you prepare for future faith-sharing opportunities? How can you rely more heavily on the Holy Spirit in them?**

Family | WE ARE FAMILY

DRAMA	Title: **CHEAPER BY THE DOZEN**	PG
	20th Century Fox, 2003	

Scripture: Genesis 2:18-24
Alternate Take: Lost Sheep (Luke 15:3-7)

DVD CHAPTER:	24
START TIME:	1 hour, 20 minutes, 45 seconds
START CUE:	The family pours out of the house.
END TIME:	1 hour, 23 minutes, 45 seconds
END CUE:	Tom and Mark hug.
DURATION:	3 minutes

Overview: The Bakers realize that Mark's missing. They scatter, scouring the city looking for him, refusing to give up. They finally find him on a train heading for Midland.

Illustration: God created this strange unit called "family" for a reason. Explore exactly the purpose of and our responsibility to the family God blessed (and I do mean blessed) us with.

Questions:

- **Do you feel like your family shares a bond similar to the Bakers? Why or why not?**
- Read Genesis 2:18-24. **In the beginning, God could have created anything he wanted. Why did he create the family?**
- **How does your family help your spiritual growth? Hinder it?**
- **What responsibilities do we have to our family, even if it's dysfunctional?**
- **What can you do this week to better fulfill those responsibilities?**

Favoritism | I LOVE YOUR BROTHER MORE

DRAMA	**Title: THE LORD OF THE RINGS: THE RETURN OF THE KING** New Line Cinema, 2003	**PG-13**

Scripture: Genesis 25:27-28
Alternate Take: Joseph (Genesis 37:3-4)

DVD CHAPTER:	18
START TIME:	59 minutes, 30 seconds
START CUE:	Denethor sits down at a table.
END TIME:	1 hour, 1 minute, 00 seconds
END CUE:	Faramir exits.
DURATION:	1 minute, 30 seconds

Overview: Denethor questions why his son Faramir would abandon the outer defenses when his brother Borimir kept them intact for years. Faramir states that his father obviously wishes Borimir had lived and he had died instead, and Denethor agrees. Faramir leaves on a suicide mission, hoping it will earn his father's love.

Illustration: Families are a source of joy, comfort…and pressure. It may never be spoken, but it's impossible not to compare ourselves to our siblings. Thankfully, God doesn't compare us to anyone in the world. He makes each of us unique and with a different purpose.

Questions:

- **How many of you compare yourself or feel compared to a sibling or friend? Why?**
- **How do the comparisons make you feel?**
- Read Genesis 25:27-28. **How do you think Esau and Jacob felt being compared?**
- **Why doesn't God compare people?**
- **How can you help your family members stop comparing each other and simply love the differences?**

Fear | WHAT'S IN THE CLOSET?

Title: **MONSTERS, INC.**	G
HUMOR Walt Disney Pictures, 2001	

Scripture: Proverbs 3:21-26
Alternate Take: Learning (Psalm 111:10)

DVD CHAPTER:	2
START TIME:	1 minute, 45 seconds
START CUE:	A kid sleeps in his bed.
END TIME:	4 minutes, 45 seconds
END CUE:	The teacher says, "Like James P. Sullivan."
DURATION:	3 minutes

Overview: A monster practices scaring a child in a simulation. His biggest mistake was leaving the door open—that could let a (toxic) kid inside his world. This thought sends the monsters into a panic.

Illustration: Fear seems to have a death-grip on our society with all the worries concerning such "monsters" as insta-death from a whiff of second-hand smoke or cancer-causing french fries. Defuse the media, encouraging your students to resist the grip of fear by resting in God's promises.

Questions:
- What kinds of things are people scared of these days?
- What is your biggest fear, and how does it impact your life?
- Read Proverbs 3:21-26. **Do you think Solomon's advice truly "cures" fear? Why or why not?**
- Is all fear unhealthy? Explain.
- What must you do differently in your life to be able to face your fears with God's help?

Flesh vs. Spirit | I DO BUT I DON'T

Title: **SPIDER-MAN**	PG-13
DRAMA Columbia Pictures, 2002	

Scripture: Galatians 5:16-25
Alternate Take: Sin Nature (Psalm 51:1-4)

DVD CHAPTER:	19
START TIME:	1 hour, 12 minutes, 15 seconds
START CUE:	Osborn pours a drink.
END TIME:	1 hour, 14 minutes, 15 seconds
END CUE:	Osborn laughs.
DURATION:	2 minutes

Themes **D-F**

Overview: Osborn talks with his evil alter ego, the Green Goblin. His split personality manifests itself—showing that half of him murders and steals while the other half stands appalled.

Illustration: Don't you have conversations like this with yourself? It seems as if the tug-of-war between flesh and spirit never ends, but that's no reason to give up. Bolster your students, encouraging them to not give up the fight. Righteousness will win in the end.

Questions:

- **What situation or temptation makes your flesh and spirit fight like this?**
- **Have your struggles between flesh and spirit grown easier or more difficult since you began following Jesus? Explain.**
- Read Galatians 5:16-25. **Why don't our fleshly desires simply disappear once we follow Christ?**
- **What exactly does it mean to "keep in step with the Spirit"?**
- **What must you start doing in order to walk daily in the Spirit?**

Forgiveness | CAN YOU?

HUMOR	Title: **BILLY MADISON**	PG-13
	Universal Pictures, 1995	

Scripture: Mark 11:25
Alternate Take: Bitterness (Hebrews 12:14-15)

DVD CHAPTER:	9
START TIME:	59 minutes, 30 seconds
START CUE:	Billy dials the phone.
END TIME:	1 hour, 00 minutes, 45 seconds
END CUE:	Danny opens some lipstick.
DURATION:	1 minute, 15 seconds

Overview: Billy calls Danny McGrath and apologizes for picking on him in high school. Danny accepts Billy's apology, hangs up, and marks his name off a "People to Kill" list.

Illustration: This clip plays both sides of the forgiveness coin—both asking for as well as granting it. Walk through this uncomfortable process (for both parties), looking ahead to the miraculous healing it brings.

Questions:

- **Does anyone come to mind from whom you need to ask forgiveness? What did you do?**
- Read Mark 11:25. **What prevents people from asking for or granting forgiveness?**
- **What makes forgiveness the cornerstone of the Christian faith and life?**
- **What do you feel led to do in light of these verses?**

Free Will | IT'S THEIR CHOICE

DRAMA

Title: BRUCE ALMIGHTY

Universal Pictures, 2003

PG-13

Scripture: Deuteronomy 11:26-28
Alternate Take: God's Love (Isaiah 49:15-16)

DVD CHAPTER:	14
START TIME:	1 hour, 7 minutes, 30 seconds
START CUE:	Bruce sits on a couch.
END TIME:	1 hour, 8 minutes, 30 seconds
END CUE:	God says, "You let me know."
DURATION:	1 minute

Overview: Bruce informs God that Grace left him. He asks how you make someone love you without affecting free will. God responds by welcoming Bruce to his life.

Illustration: Do you think God ever regrets giving us free will? Seriously, this convoluted topic can make even the most learned theologian's head spin. Give your youth a baseline knowledge of free will as it fits within their relationship with God and faith.

Questions:
- Why would God give humanity, his creation, free will?
- Read Deuteronomy 11:26-28. **Do we ever surprise God by our choices? Explain.**
- What motivates so many people to choose a curse rather than a blessing?
- What are some ways you can make sure your free will is being used to please God rather than yourself?

Friends | CUT HIM LOOSE

DRAMA

Title: MASTER AND COMMANDER: THE FAR SIDE OF THE WORLD

20th Century Fox, 2003

PG-13

Scripture: 1 Corinthians 15:33
Alternate Take: Leadership (Hebrews 3:17)

DVD CHAPTER:	15
START TIME:	50 minutes, 45 seconds
START CUE:	The mast breaks.
END TIME:	53 minutes, 15 seconds
END CUE:	Wally disappears behind a wave.
DURATION:	2 minutes, 30 seconds

Overview: Wally tries to tie up the sail when the mast breaks, throwing him overboard. The mast is sinking the ship, and the crew must cut it loose, leaving Wally to drown.

Illustration: Sometimes the bad company we keep can drag us down. We are tied to the friends we keep, and it might be time to cut the binding rope. Challenge your teens to examine their friendships objectively, deciding whether those relationships draw them closer to God or threaten to drag them down into the depths.

Questions:
- Have you ever had to cut off one of your friends because they were dragging you down? If so, what happened?
- Read 1 Corinthians 15:33. **When is it proper to label someone as "bad company"?**
- What is the balance between reaching out to people who don't know Christ and not keeping "bad company"?
- Why do people sometimes refuse to cut off a bad friend?
- Are there any friends you need to cut off? If so, how will you do that?

Fruit of the Spirit | I GOT POWERS!

DRAMA	Title: **SPIDER-MAN**	PG-13
	Columbia Pictures, 2002	

Scripture: Galatians 5:22-23
Alternate Take: New Life (2 Corinthians 5:14-17)

DVD CHAPTER:	8
START TIME:	25 minutes, 15 seconds
START CUE:	Peter runs into an alley.
END TIME:	28 minutes, 00 seconds
END CUE:	Peter slams into a wall.
DURATION:	2 minutes, 45 seconds

Overview: Peter discovers and uses his new powers—climbing walls, leaping between buildings, and slinging webs.

Illustration: People who follow Jesus have the fruit of the Spirit inside them—we just need to learn how to cultivate this fruit to bless others. Discuss the nine fruits as well as how to make this spiritual garden grow.

Questions:
- Read Galatians 5:22-23. **What "superpowers" do all Christians have inside them ready to burst out?**
- What prevents this supernatural fruit from naturally coming out of every Christian all the time?
- What are some practical ways we can cultivate our fruit?
- What one fruit do you want to focus on growing, and how will you do that?

The Future | WHAT'S AROUND THE CORNER?

	Title: **SEABISCUIT**	
DRAMA	Universal Pictures, 2003	PG-13

Scripture: Luke 12:16-21

Alternate Takes: Preparation (1 Thessalonians 5:1-6),
Tragedy (Isaiah 15:1-4)

DVD CHAPTER:	4
START TIME:	12 minutes, 45 seconds
START CUE:	A hog is placed on the table.
END TIME:	14 minutes, 30 seconds
END CUE:	"Twenty-five percent of the workforce was unemployed."
DURATION:	1 minute, 45 seconds

Overview: Howard recounts how he amassed his fortune through nothing but hard work. He believes in a bright future. As he and his friends celebrate, the stock market crashes, sending millions out of work and the nation into depression.

Illustration: No one knows the future but God. That's why it's so important to tether our life and dreams to the solid rock of his character so we don't get swept away by any unforeseen future events.

Questions:
- What excites you the most about the future? What frightens you the most?
- Read Luke 12:16-21. Is Jesus saying we shouldn't prepare for the future?
- What is the balance between planning for the future and trusting in God for your future?
- How can you keep God as your priority even when pursuing future plans?

Themes

D-F

Generational Sin | PASS IT ON DOWN

DRAMA	Title: **ANTWONE FISHER**	PG-13
	Fox Searchlight, 2002	

Scripture: Exodus 34:6-7
Alternate Takes: Anger (Ecclesiastes 7:9),
Choices (Deuteronomy 30:19-20)

DVD CHAPTER:	9
START TIME:	28 minutes, 00 seconds
START CUE:	Davenport stands by the bookshelf.
END TIME:	29 minutes, 15 seconds
END CUE:	Antwone says, "Yes, sir."
DURATION:	1 minute, 15 seconds

Overview: Davenport gives Antwone a book that explains how bad habits get passed down through generations. The Tates' actions were wrong. Just as they chose to do what's wrong, Antwone can choose to do what's right and deal with his anger constructively.

Illustration: Why must we suffer for the sins of our parents? Pull a "Dr. Davenport," and explain this harsh truth as well as biblical methods for finding a path out of the effects of the improper choices of our ancestors.

Questions:

- **What bad habits have your parents passed down to you?**
- **Why does it seem that we can't help but follow our parents' example, even when we hate it?**
- Read Exodus 34:6-7. **Does God's declaration sound very loving? Why or why not?**
- **Why must children suffer for their parents' mistakes?**
- **What must people do to break free from the "sin of the fathers"?**

Generosity | YOU HAVE IT

DRAMA	Title: **SPY KIDS 3D: GAME OVER**	PG
	Dimension Films, 2003	

Scripture: Proverbs 11:24-25
Alternate Take: Sacrifice (Acts 20:22-24)

DVD CHAPTER:	16
START TIME:	41 minutes, 45 seconds
START CUE:	Arnold says, "Don't worry, Guy."
END TIME:	43 minutes, 00 seconds

END CUE:	Demetra says, "Thank you."
DURATION:	1 minute, 15 seconds

Overview: Juni finds a life pack—a rare item that will grant him more lives. He gives it to Demetra because she needs it.

Illustration: It's rare to find genuine generosity these days. After Jesus freely gave his life for ours, we should be falling all over ourselves giving whatever we have to others. Discuss both the practical and impractical ways your youth can show generosity, helping them make it a habit as natural as breathing.

Questions:
- How did you feel the last time someone was generous to you?
- What prevents people from being more generous? What prevents you?
- Read Proverbs 11:24-25. **How have you either seen or personally experienced these verses to be true?**
- What are some ways you can be generous beyond giving away money?
- Where could you become more generous in life, and how will you implement that?

Gluttony | I CAN'T BELIEVE I ATE THE WHOLE THING

Title: **SUPER SIZE ME**		PG
DRAMA	Samuel Goldwyn Films, 2004	

Scripture: Proverbs 23:19-21
Alternate Take: Self-Control (Titus 2:11-14)

DVD CHAPTER:	1
START TIME:	1 minute, 15 seconds
START CUE:	An American flag is shown on the screen.
END TIME:	2 minutes, 30 seconds
END CUE:	"Over 400,000 deaths per year."
DURATION:	1 minute, 15 seconds

Overview: Morgan Spurlock explains how the United States is the fattest nation in the world, with over 60 percent of the adults classified as overweight or obese.

Illustration: It's quite an indictment against our nation that we pork out while the rest of the world starves. Study the spiritual dimension of our food obsession, helping your youth turn their backs on gluttony.

Questions:
- How does this information make you feel?
- How would you define *gluttony*?
- Can skinny people be gluttons? Why or why not?
- Read Proverbs 23:19-21. **What can gluttony indicate about a person's spirit?**
- How can you suppress your gluttonous tendencies?

God | I'M RIGHT BESIDE YOU!

DRAMA	Title: **FREQUENCY**
	New Line Cinema, 2000

PG-13

Scripture: Acts 17:24-28
Alternate Take: Fathers (Psalm 103:13)

DVD CHAPTER:	9
START TIME:	44 minutes, 00 seconds
START CUE:	John enters the room.
END TIME:	45 minutes, 45 seconds
END CUE:	John rides in circles.
DURATION:	1 minute, 45 seconds

Overview: John's dad teaches him how to ride a bike. Dad calms John's fears by assuring him they can do it together, promising to hold on until John says he's OK. True to his word, Dad stays right there until John's riding on his own.

Illustration: God is right there, holding your bicycle as you try to learn to ride through this thing called life. Help your students feel his presence beside them, trusting in his loving care and desire to see them succeed.

Questions:
- **How is God like the dad in this clip? How is God unlike him?**
- Read Acts 17:24-28. **If God is always there, why don't we consistently feel his presence?**
- **Why does God sometimes let us "crash our bikes"?**
- **What benefits come with being the offspring of a loving God?**
- **How can you better connect with God and feel his presence this week?**

God's Family | I DON'T TAKE THE BEST

DRAMA	Title: **MIRACLE**
	Walt Disney Pictures, 2004

PG

Scripture: Deuteronomy 7:7-8
Alternate Take: The Body of Christ (1 Corinthians 12:14-31)

DVD CHAPTER:	3
START TIME:	12 minutes, 45 seconds
START CUE:	Herb hands Craig a piece of paper.
END TIME:	14 minutes, 00 seconds
END CUE:	Herb says, "You ever see him when his game's on?"
DURATION:	1 minute, 15 seconds

Overview: Herb hands Craig a list of names—Herb's list of members for his team. Craig can't believe Herb can choose a team on the first day, especially with the best players missing from the list. Herb counters that he's not looking for the best players but the best team.

Illustration: God isn't looking for the best and brightest for his team—only hearts broken before him in humility and repentance. Remind your young people what it means to be a part of God's family.

Questions:
- Why was Herb's method for choosing a team so crazy?
- Read Deuteronomy 7:7-8. **How is membership in God's "team" similar to membership in Herb's team?**
- Why doesn't God necessarily choose the best and the brightest to be in his family?
- What attitudes and beliefs should this knowledge elicit in God's followers?

God's Guidance | WHAT SHOULD I DO?

Title: **BLUE CRUSH**

DRAMA

Universal Pictures, 2002

PG-13

Scripture: Proverbs 15:21-22
Alternate Take: Desires (Galatians 5:16-18)

DVD CHAPTER:	13
START TIME:	1 hour, 13 minutes, 00 seconds
START CUE:	Matt asks, "What do you want?"
END TIME:	1 hour, 14 minutes, 45 seconds
END CUE	Matt finishes, "…never ask a guy what to do."
DURATION:	1 minute, 45 seconds

Overview: Marie lists off her desires to Matt, finishing with wanting to win Pipe Masters. Matt tells her to do it, but she's scared she'll fail. She's confused and wants to know what to do.

Illustration: Everybody wants a heavenly map to fall out of the sky, providing direction for life. God wants us to *live* life, connecting with him for guidance in relationship rather than handing out a CliffsNotes guide. Help your students find some direction before they decide to give up and tread water.

Questions:
- Can you relate to Marie's fears? Why or why not?
- Do you have a good system for figuring out direction in your life? If so, what is it? If not, how do you decide?
- Read Proverbs 15:21-22. **What advice do these verses give for finding God's guidance in life?**
- Why doesn't God make plainly clear the direction he wants us to take?
- How can you learn to hear God's voice more clearly when seeking guidance in life?

God's Love | I'M AFTER YOU

Title: THE BOURNE SUPREMACY

DRAMA

Universal Pictures, 2004

PG-13

Scripture: Ezekiel 16:1-15
Alternate Take: God's Omniscience (Job 34:21-22)

DVD CHAPTER:	10
START TIME:	46 minutes, 30 seconds
START CUE:	Bourne walks through a revolving door.
END TIME:	49 minutes, 15 seconds
END CUE:	Landy answers her phone.
DURATION:	2 minutes, 45 seconds

Overview: Bourne tracks down Pamela Landy, figuring out the location of her hotel room and following her to work. He gains access to the roof of the building across from her offices and watches her through a rifle sight, finally getting her attention by calling.

Illustration: Challenge any perceptions of God keeping us in his sights, ready to shoot us down when we mess up. God's *love* compels him to keep a constant eye on our every move. Hopefully, understanding that intense love will inspire a desire to please our heavenly Father with every action he sees.

Questions:
- How does it make you feel to know that God is always watching you?
- Read Ezekiel 16:1-15. How do the verses express God's infinite love toward you?
- How must God feel when people ignore him, going about their lives as if he doesn't exist?
- What are some proper ways for us to respond to God's love?

God's Omniscience | MR. KNOW-IT-ALL

Title: THE SUM OF ALL FEARS

DRAMA

Paramount Pictures, 2002

PG-13

Scripture: 1 Chronicles 28:9
Alternate Take: Humanity (Acts 17:24-28)

DVD CHAPTER:	16
START TIME:	1 hour, 55 minutes, 00 seconds
START CUE:	Grushkov walks up.
END TIME:	1 hour, 57 minutes, 15 seconds
END CUE:	Grushkov walks away.
DURATION:	2 minutes, 15 seconds

Overview: Grushkov and Ryan agree to keep the back channels open. All of humanity shares a common link, so they must avert future disasters. Then Grushkov offers congratulations on Ryan's engagement. Ryan can't believe it—no one knows! Grushkov smiles and leaves.

Illustration: God knows it all. How he can be immediately aware of every intimate detail in humanity and *still* love us is a testimony to his unfathomable grace. Discuss God's perfect omniscience and what impact it has on us.

Questions:
- **How does it make you feel when someone knows something you thought was hidden?**
- Read 1 Chronicles 28:9. **What are the pros and cons of God knowing everything?**
- **Why do Christians have nothing to fear from God's omniscience?**
- **How can God love us so fiercely even though he knows everything about us?**

Gossip | TURN AROUND SO I CAN STAB YOU

Title: **BLUE CRUSH**

DRAMA   Universal Pictures, 2002   **PG-13**

Scripture: Proverbs 26:20-24
Alternate Take: Taming the Tongue (Proverbs 18:20-21)

DVD CHAPTER:	13
START TIME:	1 hour, 10 minutes, 00 seconds
START CUE:	Women enter the bathroom.
END TIME:	1 hour, 11 minutes, 15 seconds
END CUE:	A girl says, "Was that just her?"
DURATION:	1 minute, 15 seconds

Overview: A group of women talk about Marie, ripping on her clothing and job as a maid. Marie exits a stall and gives her shoes to the girl who said she liked them.

Illustration: It's amazing what a popular pastime gossip has become since it has absolutely no productive value other than creating irreparable damage to one's heart and soul. Rip the evil rumor weed out of the hearts of your youth so it doesn't eventually strangle your ministry.

Questions:
- Why do people gossip?
- How do they justify talking about other people?
- Read Proverbs 26:20-24. **Why is gossip so destructive?**
- How can it tear apart our community here?
- What must you do to strip all gossip from your lips?

Grace | I'LL GIVE YOU A SECOND CHANCE

DRAMA

Title: **MAID IN MANHATTAN**

Columbia Pictures, 2002

PG-13

Scripture: 2 Corinthians 12:8-10

Alternate Takes: Equality (Proverbs 22:2), Second Chances (John 21:15-17)

DVD CHAPTER:	27
START TIME:	1 hour, 35 minutes, 00 seconds
START CUE:	The exterior of the Roosevelt Hotel is shown on the screen.
END TIME:	1 hour, 36 minutes, 45 seconds
END CUE:	The crowd applauds.
DURATION:	1 minute, 45 seconds

Overview: Ty asks Mr. Marshall a question at the press conference. He wants to know if Mr. Marshall believes in second chances since everyone makes mistakes.

Illustration: Grace is a beautiful thing—completely undeserved but always appreciated. Discuss both God's supernatural grace for humanity as well as our duty in extending it to those around us.

Questions:
- When have you been given a second chance in life?
- How was this an act of grace?
- Read 2 Corinthians 12:8-10. **How does grace keep us humble?**
- What prevents Christians from showing grace despite Jesus' grace toward us?
- How can you learn to show more grace to the people around you?

Grades | YOU ALL GET A'S!

HUMOR

Title: **SCHOOL OF ROCK**

Paramount Pictures, 2003

PG-13

Scripture: Proverbs 13:4

Alternate Takes: Equality (Deuteronomy 10:17), God (Isaiah 1:18)

DVD CHAPTER:	3
START TIME:	13 minutes, 00 seconds
START CUE:	Summer raises her hand.
END TIME:	14 minutes, 15 seconds
END CUE:	Kids have "recess."
DURATION:	1 minute, 15 seconds

Overview: Summer asks how they can possibly chart academic progress by having recess all the time. Dewey studies the class performance chart filled with stars and demerits. He rips the chart apart, proclaiming there will be no grades.

Illustration: Thankfully, God works on a Dewey scale of no spiritual grades. In the meantime, your students must deal with those pesky letters and numbers that make up their academic records. Help them see God's plan in the midst of their GPAs."

Questions:
- How do you feel about grades in school?
- Does God care about our grades? Why or why not?
- Read Proverbs 13:4. **What does God deem more important for success than grades?**
- In light of this verse, what is your responsibility toward grades?

Greed | TOO MUCH IS NOT ENOUGH

HUMOR	Title: CHICAGO	PG-13
	Miramax Films, 2002	

Scripture: Luke 12:15-31
Alternate Take: Forgiveness (Luke 6:27-30)

DVD CHAPTER:	7
START TIME:	39 minutes, 15 seconds
START CUE:	Amos sits in a waiting room.
END TIME:	41 minutes, 00 seconds
END CUE:	Flynn sweeps the money into a drawer.
DURATION:	1 minute, 45 seconds

Overview: Flynn admires Amos for standing by Roxie. Amos sheepishly admits he doesn't have $5,000. Flynn calls Amos a liar and refuses to represent Roxie. Amos apologizes, and Flynn snatches the $2,000 Amos does have, agreeing to take the case.

Illustration: Greed fuels many decisions in life. This powerful desire doesn't figure into any of God's kingdom plans. Help your students identify any greed that lurks in their hearts and purge it from their system.

Questions:
- How would you define *greed?*
- What kinds of things can people be greedy for besides money?
- Read Luke 12:15-31. **Why is greed so empty?**
- What remedy does Jesus give for fighting greed?
- In what areas do you struggle with greed, and how will you fight it?

Happiness | MORE THAN A FEELING

DRAMA	Title: THE HOURS	PG-13
	Paramount Pictures, 2002	

Scripture: Matthew 5:1-12
Alternate Take: Meaning (Isaiah 1:17)

DVD CHAPTER:	13
START TIME:	1 hour, 13 minutes, 45 seconds
START CUE:	Julia says, "You've been crying."
END TIME:	1 hour, 16 minutes, 45 seconds
END CUE:	Clarissa says, "It was the moment. Right then."
DURATION:	3 minutes

Overview: Clarissa complains that Richard makes her life feel trivial. She admits her life does seem silly. She tells her daughter how she was her happiest years ago and thought it was the beginning of happiness. Now she knows that moment *was* the happiness—it's not coming back.

Illustration: Happiness should not be determined by external circumstances. It can be found in the heart of even the most desperate person in dire straits. Give your teenagers the wonderful gift of Christ-like happiness that can never be stolen.

Questions:
- Why do you think there are so many unhappy people?
- What was the happiest time in your life?
- Read Matthew 5:1-12. What do you think of Jesus' recipe for happiness?
- How can people be happy when the circumstances around them stink?
- What must you do to create a sense of happiness that can't be taken away?

Helping Others | DON'T TURN AWAY

DRAMA	Title: **RADIO** Columbia Pictures, 2003	**PG**

Scripture: Deuteronomy 15:7-11

Alternate Takes: Justice (Romans 2:14-16), Omission (James 4:17)

DVD CHAPTER:	23
START TIME:	1 hour, 21 minutes, 15 seconds
START CUE:	The truck parks at the house.
END TIME:	1 hour, 24 minutes, 00 seconds
END CUE:	Coach and Mary Helen exit the truck.
DURATION:	2 minutes, 45 seconds

Overview: Coach tells his daughter about his old paper route. He found a little boy his own age being held underneath a house, caged in with barbed wire. He had the route for over two years and never did anything to help the boy.

Illustration: We *must* act to help those in need when we encounter them. Challenge the teenagers in your ministry to identify those they know both personally and in passing who need tangible help. Help them find out how they can communicate the love of Christ through their actions.

Questions:

- **What are some current examples, either locally or around the world, where people have acted like Coach?**
- Read Deuteronomy 15:7-11. **Why do people harden their hearts to obvious need?**
- **Are there any limits to the amount of help we must give people? Why or why not?**
- **How have you seen the love of Christ preached mightily through simply helping other people?**
- **What are some practical ways you can help the people immediately around you in your life?**

Heroes | THEY'RE STILL OUT THERE

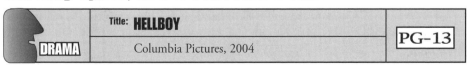

DRAMA	**Title: SPIDER-MAN 2**	**PG-13**
	Columbia Pictures, 2004	

Scripture: Hebrews 11
Alternate Take: Sacrifice (Luke 22:14-20)

DVD CHAPTER:	35
START TIME:	1 hour, 23 minutes, 15 seconds
START CUE:	Henry says, "You take Spider-Man's pictures, right?"
END TIME:	1 hour, 25 minutes, 00 seconds
END CUE:	Aunt May says, "He needs him."
DURATION:	1 minute, 45 seconds

Overview: Aunt May and Henry wonder where Spider-Man has gone. The world needs heroes who set courageous, self-sacrificing examples to the world and teach people how to live with hope and dignity. A hero is noble for giving up his dreams for the sake of others.

Illustration: Discuss the real heroes of our society—their traits, actions, beliefs—and how each one of your students can become heroic for the kingdom of God today.

Questions:

- **Whom do people hold up as heroes in our society?**
- **What qualities would you ascribe to a hero?**
- Read Hebrews 11. **Which of these "heroes" of the faith surprises you? Explain.**
- **How are the heroes in God's kingdom different from modern-day heroes?**
- **How can you build heroic qualities into your own character?**

The Holy Spirit | HE'S A CONSUMING FIRE

DRAMA	**Title: HELLBOY**	**PG-13**
	Columbia Pictures, 2004	

Scripture: Matthew 3:11-12
Alternate Take: Anger (Ephesians 4:31-32)

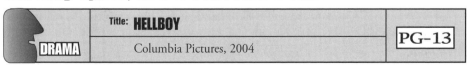

Themes G-K

DVD CHAPTER:	13
START TIME:	49 minutes, 00 seconds
START CUE:	An overhead shot of the projects.
END TIME:	50 minutes, 15 seconds
END CUE:	The hospital explodes.
DURATION:	1 minute, 15 seconds

Overview: Liz dreams of getting pelted with rocks as a child. The abuse triggers her fire-starting abilities, engulfing her body in blue flames that start a cataclysmic fire that races through the hospital.

Illustration: The Holy Spirit is a consuming fire of unimaginable power. Unfortunately, we tend to keep him bottled up like a weenie-roast campfire rather than a raging conflagration. Discuss the Holy Spirit's ministry and purpose along with ways to let his righteous fire blaze in our lives.

Questions:
- Read Matthew 3:11-12. **Do you typically think of the Holy Spirit as a raging fire? Explain.**
- **What kinds of things should we see happening when the Holy Spirit rages like a fire?**
- **What are some ways we bottle up or quench the Holy Spirit's fire?**
- **How can you stoke the Holy Spirit's fire in your life?**

Honesty | I CANNOT TELL A LIE

HUMOR	Title: **THE TERMINAL**	
	DreamWorks, 2004	PG-13

Scripture: 2 Corinthians 4:1-2
Alternate Take: Fear (Psalm 27:1-6)

DVD CHAPTER:	13
START TIME:	44 minutes, 00 seconds
START CUE:	Police remove the sandwich.
END TIME:	47 minutes, 00 seconds
END CUE:	Dixon says, "No."
DURATION:	3 minutes

Overview: Dixon tells Viktor he can leave the terminal if Viktor fears returning to his home country. Dixon asks if he's afraid to go home, and Viktor says "No." Dixon lists off the bombs, torture, and war taking place in his homeland and asks Viktor if he's scared of them. Viktor still says he's not scared to return.

Illustration: One can't help but admire Viktor's childlike honesty here. Is this the level of honesty that God requires of his followers? Talk about this virtue and how God's children must apply it to everyday life.

Questions:
- Have you ever suffered for your honesty? If so, what happened?
- What reasons do people have for lying?
- Read 2 Corinthians 4:1-2. **What makes complete honesty such a revolutionary concept that sets Christians apart?**
- Do you think Christians are known for their honesty? Why or why not?
- What must you do personally to live up to the command in these verses?

Hope | I CAN GO ON

	Title: **BARBERSHOP**	
DRAMA	MGM, 2002	PG-13

Scripture: Isaiah 40:28-31

Alternate Takes: Encouragement (1 Thessalonians 5:11), Influence (Proverbs 12:18), Standing Firm (1 Corinthians 16:13-14)

DVD CHAPTER:	16
START TIME:	46 minute, 30 seconds
START CUE:	Calvin grabs a drink.
END TIME:	48 minutes, 15 seconds
END CUE:	Calvin exits.
DURATION:	1 minute, 45 seconds

Overview: Samir thanks Calvin for his encouraging words in his time of despair. Those seemingly insignificant words were huge for him, giving him the courage to stay and rebuild his shop.

Illustration: It's amazing how easily we can spread hope through only a few words, a hug, or even a smile. Remind your young people that they have no idea what clouds loom in the lives of the people around them. Each encounter is a great chance for them to spread the hope of God that can make such a powerful difference.

Questions:
- When has someone given you hope in a hopeless situation?
- What makes an ethereal thing like hope so powerful?
- Read Isaiah 40:28-31. **How does God give his people hope?**
- What are some ways you can transfer this hope to the hurting people around you?

Identity | WHO AM I?

	Title: **THE BOURNE IDENTITY**	
DRAMA	Universal Pictures, 2002	PG-13

Scripture: Romans 8:12-17

Alternate Take: Facades (Leviticus 19:11)

DVD CHAPTER:	5
START TIME:	15 minutes, 30 seconds
START CUE:	The banker pulls back a curtain.
END TIME:	18 minutes, 00 seconds
END CUE:	Bourne exits.
DURATION:	2 minutes, 30 seconds

Overview: Jason opens his safe deposit box, learning his real name. His relief morphs into shock when he uncovers multiple passports, tons of international cash, and a pistol. Jason exits with more questions about his identity than when he entered.

Illustration: People don and discard whatever fashion, ideal, or worldview works for them at the moment. Finding one's identity in Christ brings clarity, no matter what the situation. Help your students recognize that grounding themselves in Jesus Christ provides the peace and proper foundation they need for incredible spiritual growth.

Questions:
- What kinds of things make up a person's identity?
- What are some ways people switch their identities?
- Have you ever done this? Explain.
- Read Romans 8:12-17. **How does being a child of God provide you the only identity you will ever need?**
- **In what areas can your identity in Christ bring more peace and purpose to your everyday life?**

Impatience | I WANT IT NOW

Title: STAR WARS EPISODE II: ATTACK OF THE CLONES	
DRAMA 20th Century Fox, 2002	**PG**

Scripture: Psalm 37:7
Alternate Take: Mentor (Proverbs 15:21-22)

DVD CHAPTER:	9
START TIME:	27 minutes, 45 seconds
START CUE:	Amidala enters.
END TIME:	29 minutes, 30 seconds
END CUE:	Anakin stands.
DURATION:	1 minute, 45 seconds

Overview: Amidala comments on Anakin's growth. He doesn't think Obi-Wan sees it. He feels his mentor holds him back. Amidala states that mentors see our faults and help us grow—be patient.

Illustration: "Wait 'til you're older." Tired of hearing that? Break the sad news to your teenagers that they'll be forced to wait for things their whole life. They might as well learn patience now so they can glorify God while sitting in any future holding patterns he places them in.

Questions:

- Read Psalm 37:7. **Why does God require us to wait patiently in him?**
- **How does impatience affect your attitude? your relationships?**
- **What one thing makes you the most impatient?**
- **What steps will you take to start practicing patience in this area?**

Influence | SING ALONG!

HUMOR	Title: **MR. DEEDS**	PG-13
	Columbia Pictures, 2002	

Scripture: Matthew 5:13-16
Alternate Take: Worship (Psalm 96:1-4)

DVD CHAPTER:	6
START TIME:	16 minutes, 15 seconds
START CUE:	Seder says, "I mean look at him."
END TIME:	17 minutes, 00 seconds
END CUE:	Deeds says, "Party pooper."
DURATION:	45 seconds

Overview: Deeds starts singing "Major Tom," and the pilots and Anderson join in until they're shushed by Chuck.

Illustration: What kind of influence do you exert on others? The light of Christ should shine brightly enough to draw others. Help your young people examine both their own influence on others as well as what sway others hold on them.

Questions:

- **How did Mr. Deeds demonstrate "influence"?**
- **What people and things influence you?**
- Read Matthew 5:13-16. **How are Christians supposed to influence the world?**
- **What prevents them from becoming effective salt and light?**
- **Where does God want you to become more influential, and how will you do that?**

Injustice | I'LL PRETEND I DIDN'T SEE IT

DRAMA	Title: **HOTEL RWANDA**	PG-13
	MGM, 2004	

Scripture: Isaiah 10:1-3
Alternate Take: Helping Others (1 John 3:16-18)

DVD CHAPTER:	3
START TIME:	10 minutes, 00 seconds
START CUE:	Paul approaches his gate.
END TIME:	12 minutes, 30 seconds

Themes G–K

END CUE:	Paul rolls over.
DURATION:	2 minutes, 30 seconds

Overview: Paul witnesses the forcible removal and beating of a neighbor. He does nothing, convinced he's incapable of action. That night his wife encourages him to call in some favors, but Paul refuses—those favors are for family only.

Illustration: We must not flinch in the face of injustice. God commands us to stand up for the weak and oppressed. Discuss any unjust situations in your community or around the world and how your ministry can fight for justice.

Questions:

- What is the worst injustice that you have experienced or witnessed?
- Did you fight against that injustice? Why or why not?
- Read Isaiah 10:1-3. Should we simply wait for God to bring justice? Why or why not?
- How does a person know when they are supposed to fight against injustice or simply forgive?
- How will you begin to fight against injustice in the name of God?

Inner Life | WHAT'S GOING ON INSIDE THERE?

HUMOR	Title: **HOLLYWOOD HOMICIDE** Columbia Pictures, 2003	PG-13

Scripture: Mark 4:22

Alternate Takes: Pornography (Proverbs 4:25-27),
Secrets (Jeremiah 23:23-24)

DVD CHAPTER:	9
START TIME:	25 minutes, 00 seconds
START CUE:	Joe holds a search warrant.
END TIME:	26 minutes, 45 seconds
END CUE:	A cop says, "Porno."
DURATION:	1 minute, 45 seconds

Overview: Internal Affairs opens Joe's locker and finds he hasn't cleaned it out in years. They open K.C.'s, and he's mortified when they find his numerous books on tantric sex.

Illustration: What would people find if they opened up the locker of your soul? It's not enough to keep the outside of your life clean—Jesus wants a heart, mind, and soul that match the exterior. Find biblical ways for cleaning out the locker so your students experience no embarrassment when what's hidden comes to light.

Questions:

- What would happen if everyone's inner life was a locker that other people could open?
- Why do we hide things rather than work to make our inner life match our outer life?

- Read Mark 4:22. **How does this verse make you feel?**
- **What's the point of cleaning up our inner life if God forgives us anyway?**
- **Think to yourself about what God wants you to clean out of your "locker" and what steps you will take to do it.**

Integrity | NO ONE WILL EVER KNOW

| DRAMA | Title: **BEND IT LIKE BECKHAM** Fox Searchlight, 2002 | PG-13 |

Scripture: Acts 24:14-16
Alternate Takes: Lies (Proverbs 19:9), Parents (Ephesians 6:1-4)

DVD CHAPTER:	8
START TIME:	23 minutes, 30 seconds
START CUE:	Jess and Tony walk in the park.
END TIME:	25 minutes, 00 seconds
END CUE:	Jules and Tony start playing.
DURATION:	1 minute, 30 seconds

Overview: Jess claims her parents aren't fair—she should be able to play soccer. Tony suggests she play without them knowing. Jess doesn't want to lie, but Jules convinces her to pretend she has a summer job and play while she's at "work." Her parents will never know!

Illustration: It's a mark of integrity when we remain obedient in the face of unfairness. Challenge your teenagers to build a level of integrity that always pleases God, doing what's right even when it hurts or no one on earth would even see.

Questions:
- **What would you do in this situation? Why?**
- **Is a person justified in deceiving someone who isn't being fair? Why or why not?**
- Read Acts 24:14-16. **How does our integrity affect every area of our life?**
- **What builds integrity? What destroys it?**
- **Where is your integrity wearing thin, and how can you build it back up?**

Jesus | HE'S ALWAYS THE RIGHT ANSWER

| DRAMA | Title: **THE APOSTLE** Universal Pictures, 1997 | PG-13 |

Scripture: Luke 10:38-42
Alternate Take: Witnessing (Acts 2:36-41)

DVD CHAPTER:	4
START TIME:	15 minutes, 30 seconds

START CUE:	A huge auditorium filled with people.
END TIME:	16 minutes, 45 seconds
END CUE:	Sonny marches.
DURATION:	1 minute, 15 seconds

Overview: Sonny and another preacher trade off asking questions to which the entire congregation responds, "Jesus." He also preaches the name of Jesus to a Spanish speaking audience.

Illustration: It's all about Jesus. Period. He's the one who separates Christianity from every other religion and separates humanity from the fires of hell. Wipe everything else away, focusing on the very crux of every physical and spiritual truth—God's one and only Son.

Questions:
- How would you describe Jesus to someone?
- Why does the name *Jesus* still cause such a reaction in people?
- Read Luke 10:38-42. **What did Mary choose?**
- What is distracting you from Jesus?
- What must you do to cement Jesus as the centerpiece of your life?

Jesus' Invitation | OBEYING GOD FOREMOST

Title: **LES MISÉRABLES**	
DRAMA Columbia Pictures, 1998	**PG–13**

Scripture: Revelation 3:20
Alternate Takes: Grace (Matthew 7:7-11),
Helping Others (Isaiah 58:6-10)

DVD CHAPTER:	2
START TIME:	3 minutes, 00 seconds
START CUE:	An old woman walks up.
END TIME:	4 minutes, 15 seconds
END CUE:	Valjean says, "You're going to let me inside your house?"
DURATION:	1 minute, 15 seconds

Overview: A woman encourages Valjean to knock on the church door—they won't turn him away. The bishop greets the confessed criminal with open arms, unconcerned with his dubious history.

Illustration: Every human being bears the stigma of a convict, the stain of sin in our hearts. The kind of mercy shown in this clip astonishes—especially when it's Jesus seeking entrance into *our* house, wanting to dine with *us*. When placed in that context, any hesitation to fling the door wide appears ludicrous.

Questions:
- Would you allow a stranger like this into your home? Why or why not?

- What makes allowing someone in your house and eating with him or her such an intimate action?
- Read Revelation 3:20. **Why is Jesus the one standing outside doing the knocking and not us?**
- Why does the sinless Son of God want to eat dinner with "convicted" sinners like us?
- Have you ever responded to Jesus' invitation? Why or why not?

Jesus' Love | WILL YOU BE MY BRIDE?

Title: SWEET HOME ALABAMA

DRAMA

Touchstone Pictures, 2002

PG-13

Scripture: Revelation 19:6-9
Alternate Takes: Marriage (Genesis 2:20-25),
Romance (Song of Songs 2:3-7)

DVD CHAPTER:	1
START TIME:	7 minutes, 30 seconds
START CUE:	Melanie says, "Where are we?"
END TIME:	9 minutes, 45 seconds
END CUE:	Salespeople set out engagement rings.
DURATION:	2 minutes, 15 seconds

Overview: Andrew surprises Melanie by proposing to her inside Tiffany's after hours. She's stunned and waffles but finally accepts his proposal of marriage.

Illustration: Jesus loves us and wants us to be his bride, even though we're imperfect and often hem and haw over the proposal. Remind your students of Jesus' intense, devoted love for them, and kick around ways they can return it.

Questions:
- What is the most romantic expression of love that you've ever seen?
- Read Revelation 19:6-9. **How can Jesus love sinners like you and me enough to take us as his bride?**
- Why would someone hesitate to accept his miraculous offer and return his love?
- What can you do this week to show Jesus the love he richly deserves?

Jesus' Sacrifice | HE TOOK MY PLACE

Title: I AM DAVID

DRAMA

Lions Gate Films, 2003

PG

Scripture: Romans 5:6-8
Alternate Take: Love (John 15:12-13)

DVD CHAPTER:	9
START TIME:	51 minutes, 30 seconds
START CUE:	David soaks in a claw-foot tub.
END TIME:	53 minutes, 00 seconds
END CUE:	Fade to black.
DURATION:	1 minute, 30 seconds

Overview: David remembers stealing a piece of soap. The guards lined everyone up to find the culprit. John took the soap from David, accepting the blame and deadly punishment so David might live.

Illustration: Jesus took our place, accepting the death penalty for our transgressions. Let Jesus' amazing sacrifice sink in, and then discuss the only proper response we can have to his incredible act of selflessness.

Questions:
- **Who would you willingly sacrifice your life for? Why?**
- **What makes sacrifice such a rare and beautiful thing?**
- Read Romans 5:6-8. **Did Jesus have to sacrifice himself for us? Why or why not?**
- **Why would Jesus sacrifice himself for people he knew would reject him?**
- **Are you giving Jesus the response he deserves in light of his sacrifice? Why or why not?**

Justice | YOU WON'T GET AWAY WITH THIS!

DRAMA	**Title: DAREDEVIL** 20th Century Fox, 2003	**PG-13**

Scripture: Micah 6:8

Alternate Takes: Oppression (Psalm 146:5-10), Rape (2 Samuel 13:10-20)

DVD CHAPTER:	7
START TIME:	19 minutes, 30 seconds
START CUE:	Murdock stands in court.
END TIME:	21 minutes, 00 seconds
END CUE:	The gavel strikes.
DURATION:	1 minutes, 30 seconds

Overview: Matt Murdock cross-examines Mr. Quesada, an accused rapist. Matt's acute sense of hearing gives him assurance him that Mr. Quesada is lying on the stand. Matt hopes aloud that justice will be found in the court before justice crashes upon Mr. Quesada's head with a fury.

Illustration: Examine "justice" alongside your young people. Notice how everyone despises injustice but few honestly do anything to rectify an unjust situation. On the flip side, no one wants to see justice reign supreme when they're sitting on the wrong side of the gavel. Discuss the issue until the balance between justice and mercy becomes clear.

Questions:

- **What is the last injustice you saw that made you angry?**
- **Did you do anything to fight that wrong? Explain.**
- Read Micah 6:8. **Why doesn't God intervene every time an injustice occurs on earth?**
- **What is the proper balance between extending justice or mercy to others?**
- **What can we do to see justice done as a group, and how does this show the love of Jesus to others?**

Kindness | CAN YOU SPARE A DIME?

Title: **LES MISÉRABLES**		
DRAMA	Columbia Pictures, 1998	PG-13

Scripture: Proverbs 3:3-4
Alternate Takes: Forgiveness (Matthew 5:38-48),
Heaping Coals (Proverbs 25:21-22)

DVD CHAPTER:	8
START TIME:	22 minutes, 15 seconds
START CUE:	Valjean enters the hospital ward.
END TIME:	23 minutes, 30 seconds
END CUE:	Lafitte looks at the money.
DURATION:	1 minute, 15 seconds

Overview: Valjean arranges for Lafitte to have a new life after his accident. Lafitte apologizes for hating Valjean because of his wealth. Valjean replies that everyone needs help.

Illustration: Returning kindness for an affront powerfully communicates the gospel message. In our hard-luck, get-yours-while-you-can world, it's a lost art. Help your teenagers grow the fruit of kindness in their lives, setting themselves apart from all of the hard hearts out there.

Questions:

- **What's an example of a time someone showed you kindness and it really affected you?**
- **How would you define** *kindness?*
- Read Proverbs 3:3-4. **Why does kindness bring favor?**
- **What prevents people from simply being kind to one another?**
- **What are some practical, everyday ways you can show kindness to others?**

Leadership | IT'S LONELY AT THE TOP

HUMOR

Title: DODGEBALL: A TRUE UNDERDOG STORY

20th Century Fox, 2004

PG-13

Scripture: Psalm 72:1-7
Alternate Takes: Integrity (Luke 12:2-3),
Temptation (Matthew 26:40-41)

DVD CHAPTER:	17
START TIME:	1 hour, 00 minutes, 15 seconds
START CUE:	Peter enters.
END TIME:	1 hour, 2 minutes, 45 seconds
END CUE:	Peter stares at White, thinking.
DURATION:	2 minutes, 30 seconds

Overview: White offers Peter $100,000 in exchange for the deed to his gym. He recognizes that Peter's a leader and his guys love him, but the pressure they put on him to succeed is too much.

Illustration: What makes a leader, and what exactly is his or her God-given responsibility? Discuss leadership and how we, as Christians, should receive it.

Questions:
- What makes a person a good leader? a bad leader?
- Read Psalm 72:1-7. **How does David's description of a leader differ from what the world values in a leader?**
- What mistakes have you seen Christian leaders make?
- How do these missteps create a warped view of God?
- How can you be a God-honoring leader right now?

Legalism | I'M NOT BENDING!

DRAMA

Title: THE TERMINAL

DreamWorks, 2004

PG-13

Scripture: Matthew 23:13-28
Alternate Take: Mercy (Luke 6:36)

DVD CHAPTER:	18
START TIME:	1 hour, 8 minutes, 30 seconds
START CUE:	Viktor starts talking with the Russian.
END TIME:	1 hour, 11 minutes, 00 seconds
END CUE:	Cops drag the Russian away.
DURATION:	2 minutes, 30 seconds

Overview: Dixon refuses to help a Russian's dying father because the son has no paperwork for the pills he's carrying. The desperate man gets on his knees in front of Dixon, begging for his father's life, but Dixon will not make an exception.

Illustration: This scene vividly portrays the cold, cruel heart of legalism. While God's law is unchangeable, one must readily extend grace to those who fail. The church should be known for gentleness and compassion, never for coldhearted legalism.

Questions:

- **How did this scene make you feel? Explain.**
- **Was Dixon justified in not showing mercy? Explain.**
- Read Matthew 23:13-28. **What modern examples of legalism would be similar to the ones cited by Jesus?**
- **How does legalism oppress people and strangle the gospel?**
- **How can both the church and us as individuals show mercy without compromising God's law?**

Lies | DID I SAY THAT?

Title: HOW TO LOSE A GUY IN 10 DAYS	
HUMOR	Paramount Pictures, 2003

PG-13

Scripture: Colossians 3:9-10
Alternate Take: Expectations (Luke 4:16-30)

DVD CHAPTER:	12
START TIME:	58 minutes, 30 seconds
START CUE:	Ben exits the bathroom.
END TIME:	1 hour, 00 minutes, 00 seconds
END CUE:	Ben and Andie walk past a TV showing the Knicks game.
DURATION:	1 minute, 30 seconds

Overview: Ben lies to Andie about having to work that night—he won't even have time to watch the Knicks. Andie's sad because she has tickets. Ben changes his tune, assuming she has tickets to the basketball game. To his horror, they go see a Celine Dion concert.

Illustration: Honesty truly is the best policy, even when white lies appear to be the best path for personal gain. Confront your youth, challenging them to strive for truth in all situations.

Questions:

- **What happened the last time you got busted in a lie?**
- **Why didn't you simply tell the truth?**
- **What damage have you experienced from lies?**
- Read Colossians 3:9-10. **How does this "new self" we have put on prevent us from lying?**
- **How can you learn to overcome the temptation to lie in the future?**

Life | I DON'T MIND RISKING YOURS

Title: LARA CROFT TOMB RAIDER: THE CRADLE OF LIFE

DRAMA

Paramount Pictures, 2003

PG-13

Scripture: Acts 17:24-28
Alternate Take: Abortion (Jeremiah 1:5)

DVD CHAPTER:	16
START TIME:	1 hour, 4 minutes, 00 seconds
START CUE:	Men surround Lara.
END TIME:	1 hour, 5 minutes, 00 seconds
END CUE:	Lara moans in pain.
DURATION:	1 minute

Overview: Reiss and his men capture Lara. She warns against opening Pandora's Box. Reiss wants to wipe out most of humanity while giving the elite an antidote. He believes the world is better off with fewer people.

Illustration: It's disgusting what small regard some people have for life, whether it be toward the elderly, unborn babies, or the person who wears a pair of sports shoes they want. Point out God's view on life and our responsibility to keep it sacred.

Questions:
- **What cavalier attitudes have you seen people take toward life?**
- **Do you believe some deaths are more tragic than others? Explain.**
- Read Acts 17:24-28. **What makes life sacred and precious?**
- **How does it demean God when people regard life so flippantly?**
- **What can you do personally to protect the sanctity of life?**

Listening | YOU SAY SOMETHING?

Title: SCARY MOVIE 3

HUMOR

Dimension Films, 2003

PG-13

Scripture: Ezekiel 3:4-7
Alternate Take: Aliens (Ezekiel 1:15-20)

DVD CHAPTER:	2
START TIME:	6 minutes, 00 seconds
START CUE:	"Morning News 8" is shown on the screen.
END TIME:	6 minutes, 30 seconds
END CUE:	Cindy looks at the camera, shocked.
DURATION:	30 seconds

Overview: Cindy reports on the appearance of a crop circle. She turns the news back over to her co-anchor, who states he wasn't listening.

Illustration: If listening is an art, it ranks below Popsicle-stick sculptures on most people's scale of importance. God wants us to turn this forgotten skill into second nature, both with him and others. Find ways to make the transition from broadcast to send and receive.

Questions:
- **Would other people describe you as a good listener? Why or why not?**
- **What makes listening difficult?**
- Read Ezekiel 3:4-7. **Why do we consistently refuse to listen to God?**
- **What does it take to improve your listening skills?**
- **How would listening improve your relationships with others? with God?**

Loneliness | CAN YOU SEE ME?

Title: **CHICAGO**		
DRAMA	Miramax Films, 2002	PG-13

Scripture: Psalm 68:5-6
Alternate Takes: Self-Worth (Matthew 6:26), Uniqueness (Psalm 139:13-16)

DVD CHAPTER:	12
START TIME:	1 hour, 9 minutes, 30 seconds
START CUE:	Roxie rides off in an ambulance.
END TIME:	1 hour, 11 minutes, 15 seconds
END CUE	A newspaper is shown on the screen.
DURATION:	1 minute, 45 seconds

Overview: Amos sings about how even the most inconsequential people get noticed sometimes, but he's invisible, and no one realizes he's even alive.

Illustration: God created us for community, which might explain why loneliness hurts so much. Tear the curtains from your students' eyes, helping the popular see and respond with compassion toward the lonely around them, and helping each silently suffering "Amos" break free from isolation.

Questions:
- **When do you feel the loneliest?**
- **What are some other reasons people feel lonely?**
- Read Psalm 68:5-6. **If these verses are true, why do people experience loneliness?**
- **How does loneliness harm a person's relationship with God?**
- **What can you do to fight your own or someone else's loneliness?**

Love | I'LL DO ANYTHING

Title: **BIG FISH**		
HUMOR	Columbia Pictures, 2003	PG-13

Scripture: John 15:12-13
Alternate Take: Jacob (Genesis 29:15-20)

DVD CHAPTER:	13
START TIME:	54 minutes, 30 seconds
START CUE:	Ed says, "Wait! Look, I'll work night and day for you."
END TIME:	56 minutes, 45 seconds
END CUE:	Motorcycles race around Ed.
DURATION:	2 minutes, 15 seconds

Overview: Ed agrees to work without pay for Mr. Calloway in exchange for information on the woman he loves. He shovels elephant dung, gets shot out of a cannon, and puts his head in the mouth of a lion in his quest.

Illustration: I don't care what anybody says—that's love. Tear apart the fake versions of love the media pawns off as real and uncover the genuine article that the Author of true love created for us to enjoy.

Questions:

- Do you think Edward's actions show genuine love? Why or why not?
- Why is there so much confusion over the nature of love and what it really looks like?
- Read John 15:12-13. What does Jesus' definition tell you about the true nature of love?
- Why doesn't he include the words *romance* or *mutual attraction*?

Materialism | BUT I NEED IT!

Title: **UPTOWN GIRLS**	
HUMOR MGM, 2003	**PG-13**

Scripture: Proverbs 23:4-5
Alternate Take: Needs (Luke 12:27-34)

DVD CHAPTER:	15
START TIME:	35 minutes, 45 seconds
START CUE:	Ray takes a pill.
END TIME:	37 minutes, 15 seconds
END CUE:	Ingrid finishes, "...find our center."
DURATION:	1 minute, 30 seconds

Overview: Molly can't bear to part with any of the belongings she's trying to sell. Ingrid reminds her to stick with the essentials and sell everything else. Molly tells herself it's good to shed, but then tries to buy back what she's sold.

Illustration: It's amazing how hard it is to part with even the most useless piece of property once it comes into our possession. Do a heart check with your students, helping them identify where their stuff possesses them and discovering ways to find freedom from materialism's grip.

Questions:

- Can you relate to Molly's struggle? Why or why not?
- What other effects can materialism have on a person?
- Read Proverbs 23:4-5. Is the best defense against materialism not owning anything? Why or why not?

- At what point does a person have a problem with materialism?
- How can you purge your heart of any materialistic attitudes?

Media Messages | IT MUST BE TRUE IF IT'S ON TV

DRAMA	Title: **K-19: THE WIDOWMAKER**
	Paramount Pictures, 2002

PG-13

Scripture: 2 Peter 2:1-3
Alternate Take: Materialism (1 John 2:15-17)

DVD CHAPTER:	4
START TIME:	31 minutes, 15 seconds
START CUE:	Old newsreel footage is shown on the screen.
END TIME:	32 minutes, 30 seconds
END CUE:	A house explodes.
DURATION:	1 minute, 15 seconds

Overview: The crew watches American newsreel footage of decadence and racial hatred. An officer explains that American propaganda never reveals the greed and suffering below the glitzy surface.

Illustration: It's imperative we let our young people know they can't believe everything they see or read in the media. Not that they need to become cynical skeptics, but they must run everything through a biblical filter to look for both the spiritual truth and the lies.

Questions:
- What's the biggest lie you've seen reported in the media?
- Do you think our modern media serves as propaganda? Why or why not?
- Read 2 Peter 2:1-3. Do you think these verses can be applied to the media?
- How can a person discern the truth in the messages the media sends out?

Mental Illness | PEOPLE THINK I'M ODD

DRAMA	Title: **THE AVIATOR**
	Miramax Films, 2004

PG-13

Scripture: Exodus 4:11
Alternate Takes: Sin (Psalm 51:1-4), Works (Ephesians 2:8-9)

DVD CHAPTER:	20
START TIME:	1 hour, 26 minutes, 45 seconds
START CUE:	Howard enters the bathroom.
END TIME:	1 hour, 28 minutes, 30 seconds
END CUE:	Howard slips out of the bathroom.
DURATION:	1 minute, 45 seconds

Themes L-O

Overview: Howard scrubs his hand so hard, he cuts himself. He notices some blood on his shirt and attempts to clean that as well. When he finally finishes, there are no towels left for him to cover the doorknob. He waits, unable to touch the doorknob.

Warning: There is cursing at 1:26:47. To avoid this, begin the clip at 1:26:50.

Illustration: Why are some people born...different? Discuss God's plan in the midst of obvious mental deficiencies and how we can show his love to even the most unique personalities.

Questions:
- What are some other kinds of disabilities, both mental and physical, that a person might have?
- Read Exodus 4:11. Is God cruel for allowing people to have disabilities? Why or why not?
- What does a person's treatment of the disabled say about his or her relationship with God?
- How can we become more accommodating and loving toward people with disabilities in our ministry?

Mercy | I'M FREE?

Title: LES MISÉRABLES	
DRAMA	Columbia Pictures, 1998

PG-13

Scripture: John 3:16-18
Alternate Take: Redemption (Galatians 3:9-14)

DVD CHAPTER:	4
START TIME:	6 minutes, 45 seconds
START CUE:	Valjean removes a box from the bureau.
END TIME:	9 minutes, 45 seconds
END CUE:	Valjean and the priest stare at each other.
DURATION:	3 minutes

Overview: The priest discovers Valjean stealing the silver, and Valjean knocks him out. The next day, the police drag Valjean before the priest, who claims he gave the silver as a gift, chastising the criminal for leaving the candlesticks. He tells a stunned Valjean that he's been bought for God.

Illustration: What a beautiful picture of the transformative mercy Christ offers each and every one of us—guilty sinners. Explore mercy, both how we can receive it as well as offer it to others.

Questions:
- How does it feel to receive mercy?
- When is it proper to be merciful and when must justice be served?
- Read John 3:16-18. Why doesn't the whole world receive mercy if Jesus didn't come to judge?

- **What must happen for mercy to be given? for it to be received?**
- **How does God want you to become more merciful?**

Miracles | DO THEY STILL HAPPEN?

	Title: JOSHUA	
DRAMA	Artisan, 2002	G

Scripture: Acts 20:7-12
Alternate Takes: Death (1 Corinthians 15:52-57), Lazarus (John 11:32-44)

DVD CHAPTER:	18
START TIME:	1 hour, 00 minutes, 30 seconds
START CUE:	Theo hangs a bell in the tower.
END TIME:	1 hour, 3 minutes, 30 seconds
END CUE:	"What just happened here?"
DURATION:	3 minutes

Overview: Theo falls 40 feet from the steeple and dies. Joshua talks to him, bringing him back to life.

Illustration: Does God still perform miracles? Broach this question with your youth, seeking to open their eyes to what God is doing around them at this very moment.

Questions:
- **Have you ever witnessed a miracle? If so, what happened?**
- **Why don't we see miracles happening more often?**
- Read Acts 20:7-12. **Do you think people would flock to church if something like this happened here? Explain.**
- **What is the purpose of miracles?**
- **What can you do to become more aware of possible miracles?**

Missions | HELP THE SAVAGES

	Title: RABBIT-PROOF FENCE	
DRAMA	Miramax Films, 2002	PG-13

Scripture: Matthew 28:16-20
Alternate Takes: Equality (1 Corinthians 12:22-25),
Racism (Colossians 3:9-11)

DVD CHAPTER:	4
START TIME:	12 minutes, 00 seconds
START CUE:	A slide show of "half-caste" people is shown on the screen.
END TIME:	14 minutes, 00 seconds
END CUE:	Neville finishes, "...the native must be helped."
DURATION:	2 minutes

Themes L-O

Overview: Neville presents the plight of "half-caste" Aborigines. He believes they can "breed out" all traces of their native origins and be retrained and integrated into white culture.

Illustration: It's important to establish the correct attitude when entering the mission field, whether for a weekend or a lifetime. Clearly define the purpose of and proper attitude in missions as well as how to most effectively communicate the gospel to other cultures.

Questions:

- Are Neville's intentions bad? Why or why not? Are his actions? Why or why not?
- How do Christians sometimes mirror Neville's attitude toward missions?
- Read Matthew 28:16-20. **Why doesn't Jesus command us to spread culture or democracy or morals?**
- **How does one know the difference between the message of the gospel and his or her own cultural bias?**
- **What attitudes must you develop so that you enter future mission projects with the proper perspective?**

Mistakes | IF I COULD ONLY CHANGE TIME

| DRAMA | Title: **X2: X-MEN UNITED** 20th Century Fox, 2003 | PG-13 |

Scripture: Psalm 51:1-4
Alternate Takes: Bullies (Zechariah 7:8-10),
Smoking (1 Corinthians 3:16-17)

DVD CHAPTER:	4
START TIME:	9 minutes, 30 seconds
START CUE:	A bully says, "Can I have a light?"
END TIME:	11 minutes, 15 seconds
END CUE:	Xavier says, "The next time you feel like showing off, don't."
DURATION:	1 minute, 45 seconds

Overview: Two bullies ask Pyro for a light, and he refuses. They steal his lighter, and Pyro makes the cigarette burst into flames. One bully's arm catches on fire, and Iceman freezes him. Suddenly everyone stops moving—frozen in time.

Warning: *Several seconds before this clip begins, the bullies curse twice. In order to miss this, start the clip at 9:32.*

Illustration: Don't you wish you could freeze time and fix your mistakes? Though that option isn't available, you *can* turn to Christ for help in overcoming any sin you commit. Remind your youth that their sins and blunders don't spell doom but instead are the opportunity to seek divine aid.

Questions:

- **What mistake would you change if you could freeze time and fix it?**
- **What are some ways people react to their personal mistakes?**
- Read Psalm 51:1-4. **What makes David's method for dealing with sin the best?**

- Why must we still deal with consequences if God forgives our mistakes?
- What mistake are you struggling with and how will you turn it over to God?

Modesty | YOU LOOK NICE...FOR A TRAMP

HUMOR	Title: **MRS. DOUBTFIRE**	PG-13
	20th Century Fox, 1993	

Scripture: 1 Timothy 2:9-10
Alternate Take: Honesty (Ephesians 4:14-15)

DVD CHAPTER:	18
START TIME:	1 hour, 26 minutes, 15 seconds
START CUE:	The exterior of a house is shown on the screen.
END TIME:	1 hour, 27 minutes, 30 seconds
END CUE:	Mrs. Doubtfire hangs up the dress.
DURATION:	1 minute, 15 seconds

Overview: Miranda asks Mrs. Doubtfire's opinion on which dress to wear. Mrs. Doubtfire says both choices are trashy—she should wear a frock instead. Miranda decides on the short dress anyway.

Illustration: Modesty seems to be lost in a haze of halter tops and short shorts. Even if society doesn't value modesty, God does, and his children should, too. Help your students find the line where fashionable modesty resides.

Questions:
- Do you think dressing modestly is important or valuable? Explain.
- Read 1 Timothy 2:9-10. **How does someone determine what is modest since fashion changes all the time?**
- Why is it our responsibility to worry about how others react to our clothing?
- How would you define modest dress for women? for men?
- What wardrobe changes do you need to make?

Music | LET'S GET THE WHOLE WORLD TO SING

DRAMA	Title: **THE ALAMO**	PG-13
	Touchstone Pictures, 2004	

Scripture: Psalm 98
Alternate Take: Peace (Matthew 5:9)

DVD CHAPTER:	13
START TIME:	1 hour, 27 minutes, 15 seconds
START CUE:	Davy says, "I just figured it out."
END TIME:	1 hour, 30 minutes, 00 seconds
END CUE:	The Mexican army marches in front of the Alamo.
DURATION:	2 minutes, 45 seconds

Overview: The Mexican army plays its "pre-bombardment" march. Davy scales the wall and adds some lively harmony with his fiddle. Everyone, Mexicans included, listens. When the music fades, the Texans are astonished that the Mexicans don't fire.

 Leader Tip: *The opening line in this clip is "God, I despise that tune." You could use this curse as an opportunity to discuss people's tendency to take something good and make it profane—just as music can be abused, so can God's name.*

Illustration: There is a definite spiritual power within music that can be used to glorify God...or promote destructive desires. Explore the spiritual side of music and its effects, and how your young people can discern between tunes that turn hearts toward God and away from God.

Questions:
- How have you experienced the power of music?
- Why does music have such a spiritual impact?
- Read Psalm 98. **What insights does this chapter give you into the nature and purpose of music?**
- What are some ways that music is misused?
- How might you need to change your music-listening choices?

Needs | YOU CAN'T ALWAYS GET WHAT YOU WANT

	Title: **BRUCE ALMIGHTY**	**PG-13**
HUMOR	Universal Pictures, 2003	

 Scripture: Luke 12:22-31
 Alternate Take: Miracles (Matthew 16:1-4)

DVD CHAPTER:	15
START TIME:	1 hour, 17 minutes, 45 seconds
START CUE:	Bruce and God mop the floor.
END TIME:	1 hour, 19 minutes, 00 seconds
END CUE:	The light ignites.
DURATION:	1 minute, 15 seconds

Overview: God claims you can clean anything up. Bruce made a mess by giving people what they wanted—not what they needed. People expect God to constantly perform miracles, but he says they naturally occur when ordinary people make good choices.

Illustration: Deep down, we all know that our wants don't often line up with our needs, even if we don't want to admit it. Thankfully, we can access the Spirit of God and discern the difference between wants and needs before we get disappointed. Help your youth locate this pulse for themselves.

Questions:
- Do you agree with what "God" is saying in this clip? Why or why not?
- Read Luke 12:22-31. **Why do we worry so much about wants when God promises to provide all our needs?**

- How can this promise be true when there are naked and starving people in the world?
- What specific wants do you need to let go?
- How would releasing your wants free your life and time?

Noise | JUST BE QUIET!

| | **HUMOR** | Title: **WATERWORLD** | **PG-13** |
| | | Universal Pictures, 1995 | |

Scripture: Matthew 6:6-8
Alternate Take: Listening (Psalm 81:8-14)

DVD CHAPTER:	6
START TIME:	1 hour, 9 minutes, 00 seconds
START CUE:	Mariner puts some fish on the fire.
END TIME:	1 hour, 10 minutes, 00 seconds
END CUE:	Mariner says, "Eyeball?"
DURATION:	1 minute

Overview: Enola stops singing when Mariner glares at her. He asks if she ever listens. He claims she can't hear the sound of the world because she's always making noise and moving around.

Illustration: Cell phones, TV, Internet—the list keeps growing. With all of the noise, it's no wonder we can't hear God's still, small voice. Identify all the sources of noise in life, and find ways for your teenagers to turn down the volume so they can clearly hear God.

Questions:
- Do you enjoy silence? Why or why not?
- What kinds of things cause "noise" in our lives?
- Read Matthew 6:6-8. **How does a lack of silence affect a person's spiritual life?**
- How can silence draw you closer to God?
- What sources of noise do you need to cut back on or eliminate?

Obedience | I KNOW WHAT DAD SAID, BUT...

| | **DRAMA** | Title: **RAISE YOUR VOICE** | **PG** |
| | | New Line Cinema, 2004 | |

Scripture: Ephesians 6:1-3
Alternate Take: Peer Pressure (1 Corinthians 15:33)

DVD CHAPTER:	4
START TIME:	10 minutes, 00 seconds
START CUE	A full moon is shown on the screen.

END TIME:	11 minutes, 00 seconds
END CUE:	Aunt Nina shakes her head.
DURATION:	1 minute

Overview: Terri gives her brother a graduation present—Three Days Grace tickets. He's stoked until he realizes he's grounded. She coaxes him to sneak out with her anyway.

Illustration: God doesn't care about sacrifices or intentions, only obedience. Challenge your youth to strive for a level of obedience to both God and others that can't be swayed by peer pressure or selfish whims.

Questions:

• When was the last time you disobeyed your parents? What happened?
• When do you find it most difficult to obey God or your parents?
• Read Ephesians 6:1-3. Why does God give a promise with the command to obey?
• Why should we bother obeying God if he promises to forgive us?
• What must you change in order to become more obedient?

Obesity | WILL THEY STOP STARING?

DRAMA	Title: **WHAT'S EATING GILBERT GRAPE**	PG-13
	Paramount Pictures, 1993	

Scripture: Romans 14:10-13
Alternate Take: Judging (John 7:24)

DVD CHAPTER:	8
START TIME:	1 hour, 7 minutes, 00 seconds
START CUE:	Arnie and the family exit the courthouse.
END TIME:	1 hour, 8 minutes, 15 seconds
END CUE:	The car drives down the highway.
DURATION:	1 minute, 15 seconds

Overview: The Grape family exits the courthouse, and a crowd gathers to gawk and snicker at Mama, who is morbidly overweight. The family rides home in silence.

Illustration: Obesity is becoming more common, along with the acceptability of marginalizing the people who suffer from it. Help your students see obese people through God's loving eyes, reminding them to show compassion at all times.

Questions:

• How are obese people judged in our society? in the church?
• Read Romans 14:10-13. Why is it unacceptable to treat obese people differently from others?
• What needs to change in your attitude and our ministry so all people, no matter what their weight, feel loved and accepted?
• What are some practical, loving ways Christians can help obese people deal with the challenges of their weight?

Pain | THAT LEFT A MARK

DRAMA

Title: BEND IT LIKE BECKHAM

Fox Searchlight, 2002

PG-13

Scripture: Psalm 6
Alternate Take: Appearances (1 Samuel 17:40-49)

DVD CHAPTER:	7
START TIME:	18 minutes, 00 seconds
START CUE:	The girls train with soccer balls.
END TIME:	20 minutes, 00 seconds
END CUE:	Joe and Jess leave the stands.
DURATION:	2 minutes

Overview: Jess refuses to play soccer out of embarrassment over the massive burn scars on her leg. Joe reveals his own horrible knee operation scar from an injury that prevents him from ever playing again. Joe says no one else will care about Jess' scar, so she should get out there and play the game she loves.

Illustration: Everyone has scars, the emotional kind that cut deep. No matter what caused the scar, all can be healed under Christ's gentle hands. Exposing our pain to the light prevents a person from suffering alone in silence and speeds the rejuvenation of the soul. The sooner a person seeks out healing, the speedier his or her recovery and return to the game.

Questions:
- **How can emotional pain cut deeper and last longer than any physical scar?**
- **How do emotional scars affect a person on a daily basis?**
- Read Psalm 6. **Does crying out to God automatically take away your pain? Why or why not?**
- **In what ways does sharing your hurts with other people help you deal with emotional pain?**
- **If you have emotional scars, how will you go about finding healing for them?**

Parents | I'M NOTHING LIKE THEM

DRAMA

Title: PIRATES OF THE CARIBBEAN: THE CURSE OF THE BLACK PEARL

Walt Disney Pictures, 2003

PG-13

Scripture: Exodus 20:12
Alternate Take: Sin Nature (Romans 7:14-25)

DVD CHAPTER:	7
START TIME:	48 minutes, 15 seconds
START CUE:	The Interceptor is sailing.
END TIME:	50 minutes, 30 seconds

P-R

Themes

END CUE:	Jack says, "Tortuga."
DURATION:	2 minutes, 15 seconds

Overview: Jack describes Will's father as a good man and pirate. Will claims his dad was a merchant sailor, not a pirate. Jack informs Will that his dad *was* a pirate *and* a good man. Will needs to accept that and the fact he has pirate blood in his veins.

Illustration: We can't choose our parents, but we *can* choose how we respond to them. God gives a clear command and consequence for honoring one's parents. Discuss with your young people what that looks like in practical, everyday living so they can reap their heavenly reward.

Questions:
- Are you proud of your parents? Explain.
- Why does God burden children with their parents' baggage?
- Read Exodus 20:12. **How exactly do you honor parents with whom have a poor relationship?**
- Why are we responsible for honoring a parent who might not deserve honor?
- What needs to change in your attitude so you can better honor your parents?

Peace | CAN'T WE ALL JUST GET ALONG?

HUMOR	Title: **MALIBU'S MOST WANTED**	PG-13
	Warner Brothers, 2003	

Scripture: Ecclesiastes 4:1-6
Alternate Take: Unity (Malachi 2:8-10)

DVD CHAPTER:	4
START TIME:	11 minutes, 15 seconds
START CUE:	Aid says, "We've got that cued up."
END TIME:	12 minutes, 00 seconds
END CUE:	Gluckman hangs on the rim.
DURATION:	45 seconds

Overview: A political commercial shows two gang members fighting. Gluckman appears, telling them to stop worrying about who they roll with and just be brothers. The gang bangers shake hands and play basketball together.

Illustration: Can't we all just drink a Coke, sing a song, and get along? Peace is always the ideal. Unfortunately, it's a difficult thing to achieve in a fallen world. Discuss the real-world methods and spiritual possibilities to use for bringing about peace.

Questions:
- Why isn't it this easy to bring peace to the world?
- Why do conflicts even erupt if everyone prefers peace?
- Read Ecclesiastes 4:1-6. **What hope of peace do we have in light of these verses?**
- Why should we continue to strive for peace even if perfect peace will only return with Jesus?

Perception | I'VE HEARD ABOUT YOU PEOPLE!

	Title: **MONSTERS, INC.**	
HUMOR	Walt Disney Pictures, 2001	G

Scripture: John 7:24

Alternate Take: Stereotypes (John 8:15-16)

DVD CHAPTER:	14
START TIME:	31 minutes, 00 seconds
START CUE:	Toys cover the floor.
END TIME:	32 minutes, 15 seconds
END CUE:	Mike says, "...while I think of a plan!"
DURATION:	1 minute, 15 seconds

Overview: Mike and Sulley cower in the face of Mary. Mike is convinced the little girl is dangerous, intent on finding a way to kill them.

Illustration: It's funny how our perceptions can so completely distort reality. At the same time, a spiritual perception of any situation can give insight into the true reality lurking beneath the surface. Unpack perception and how to properly use it so the world will come into sharper focus for your students.

Questions:

• What happened the last time you had a misperception?

• Read John 7:24. **What should we base our perceptions on, if not by "mere appearances"?**

• How can perception hurt the movement of the gospel? Help it?

• What are some practical ways you can hone your sense of perception?

Perfection | IS IT IN YOU?

	Title: **FRIDAY NIGHT LIGHTS**	
DRAMA	Universal Pictures, 2004	PG-13

Scripture: James 1:2-4

Alternate Takes: Christ-Likeness (1 Thessalonians 1:6-7),
Reputation (1 Timothy 3:7)

DVD CHAPTER:	3
START TIME:	10 minutes, 45 seconds
START CUE:	Camera pans down to the team kneeling on the field.
END TIME:	11 minutes, 30 seconds
END CUE:	Gaines says, "Can you be perfect?"
DURATION:	45 seconds

P-R

Themes

Overview: Coach Gaines challenges his team to think about their responsibility in protecting the team and the town. They have a reputation, and they must uphold it by winning and striving for perfection.

Illustration: Can we be perfect as Christians? It's a legitimate question that will undoubtedly spark some spirited discussion. What are you waiting for? Ask them!

Questions:

- **Can we be perfect as Christians? Why or why not?**
- **What are some improper motivations for achieving perfection or being "complete"? What are some Christ-like ones?**
- Read James 1:2-4. **Why does James give a recipe for perfection if it's impossible to achieve?**
- **Why should we strive for spiritual perfection no matter our chance of success?**
- **What will you start doing this week in your pursuit to "complete" your faith?**

Perseverance | KEEP MOVING FORWARD

Title: **THE LORD OF THE RINGS: THE TWO TOWERS**	
DRAMA	New Line Cinema, 2002	PG-13

Scripture: Romans 8:24-31

Alternate Takes: Good (Romans 8:28), Hope (Hebrews 11:1)

DVD CHAPTER:	50
START TIME:	2 hours, 44 minutes, 30 seconds
START CUE:	Frodo says, "I can't do this, Sam."
END TIME:	2 hours, 46 minutes, 45 seconds
END CUE:	Frodo and Sam stare at each other.
DURATION:	2 minutes, 15 seconds

Overview: Sam encourages a downtrodden Frodo. He remembers the great stories of old, filled with darkness and danger. The darkness was always conquered in these tales. He insists people must press forward, holding on to the belief that good does exist in the world and that it's worth fighting for.

Illustration: It's easy to descend with Frodo into discouragement these days. Thankfully we serve a God big enough to overpower any challenge, no matter how daunting or evil. Challenge your young people to take on Sam's attitude, holding on to the promises of Scripture, believing that God's good will shall be done.

Questions:

- **What situation do you see in the world that seems hopeless?**
- **How does persevering in the fight for good show people the love of God, no matter how hopeless the situation?**
- Read Romans 8:24-31. **Do these verses bring you comfort? Explain.**
- **What kinds of things can make it difficult for you to cling to your faith?**
- **What are some tangible things that you can cling to that will help you persevere through dark times?**

Pity | YOU POOR THING

DRAMA

Title: **X2: X-MEN UNITED**	
20th Century Fox, 2003	**PG-13**

Scripture: Mark 9:17-27
Alternate Takes: Anger (James 1:19-20), Faith (1 Peter 1:6-9)

DVD CHAPTER:	21
START TIME:	57 minutes, 30 seconds
START CUE:	Storm walks to the back of the ship.
END TIME:	59 minutes, 15 seconds
END CUE:	Nightcrawler says, "So can faith."
DURATION:	1 minute, 45 seconds

Overview: Storm interrupts Nightcrawler's prayers to ask about his tattoos. He says they're angelic symbols—one tattoo for each sin. He continues to explain that people fear him, but he pities them because they only see him with their eyes. Storm says she doesn't pity people because anger fuels her survival. Nightcrawler counters, "So can faith."

Illustration: The word *pity* has such a negative connotation in the world today. Rescue pity as a genuine emotion from the PC dustbin and instill a healthy sense of Christ-like pity in your students that will encourage them to change the world.

Questions:
- **Do you relate more to Nightcrawler or Storm concerning pity in this scene? Explain.**
- **Why does the word *pity* tend to have a negative connotation?**
- Read Mark 9:17-27. **What is the proper meaning of *pity*?**
- **What prevents people from having constructive pity for others?**
- **What is the proper attitude and actions that should accompany pity?**

Possessions | WHAT I MOST PRIZE

HUMOR

Title: **TWO BROTHERS**	
Universal Pictures, 2004	**PG**

Scripture: Luke 12:32-34
Alternate Take: Animals (Psalm 8:6-8)

DVD CHAPTER:	15
START TIME:	1 hour, 8 minutes, 45 seconds
START CUE:	A man brings in a red leather box.
END TIME:	1 hour, 9 minutes, 30 seconds
END CUE:	Tiger prowls inside its cage.
DURATION:	45 seconds

Overview: His excellency shows an extravagant diamond studded necklace to his wife, stating his father believed nothing was too exotic or extravagant for those he loved. She's confused when he sends the jewelry case away. Then we see the necklace on a tiger.

Illustration: Though this scene appears utterly ridiculous, it's not far from our true feelings about some of our possessions. Do you place too much value on your stuff? Find out if your students are giving diamond necklaces to the wrong things and help them refocus their energy on more worthy subjects.

Questions:

- **What are some ridiculous things you've seen people do with their possessions?**
- Read Luke 12:32-34. **Does Jesus mean we should literally sell our possessions? Explain.**
- **How can possessions bring discontent and distract us from God?**
- **How can people know if they hold on to their possessions too tightly?**
- **What physical and spiritual adjustments must you make in regard to your possessions?**

Praise Music | GIVE ME A BEAT

	Title: **THE FIGHTING TEMPTATIONS**	
HUMOR	Paramount Pictures, 2003	**PG-13**

Scripture: John 4:22-24
Alternate Take: Tradition (1 Corinthians 11:3-7)

DVD CHAPTER:	13
START TIME:	1 hour, 17 minutes, 00 seconds
START CUE:	Choir sings "Down by the Riverside."
END TIME:	1 hour, 20 minutes, 00 seconds
END CUE:	The reverend says, "I expect you to be there, too."
DURATION:	3 minutes

Overview: The choir rehearses a traditional version of "Down by the Riverside." Suddenly the kids kick in with a hip-hop beat and a righteous rap. Reverend Lewis says he doesn't care as long as they're praising God's name.

Illustration: Everyone agrees that singing praises to God is good, but opinions diverge wildly over the style of music to use. Talk about worship music with your young people, helping them move past the instruments to the heart of what it means to praise God in song. Authentic worship in "spirit and in truth" always pleases God, no matter what the tune.

Questions:

- **Which style of music did you like better? Why?**
- **What are some arguments you've heard about praise music? What is your opinion?**
- Read John 4:22-24. **How do people know if they are following the criteria for praise given in these verses?**
- **What are some ways people worship that aren't "in spirit and in truth," and how can you avoid falling into this trap?**

• What can you do to become more focused—to worship in spirit and truth while singing praises to God?

Prayer | WHAT DO I SAY?

	Title: **BRUCE ALMIGHTY**	
HUMOR	Universal Pictures, 2003	**PG-13**

Scripture: Matthew 6:5-15
Alternate Take: Selflessness (Philippians 2:3-4)

DVD CHAPTER:	18
START TIME:	1 hour, 26 minutes, 30 seconds
START CUE:	Bruce arrives in heaven.
END TIME:	1 hour, 29 minutes, 00 seconds
END CUE:	Bruce and God say, "It's good."
DURATION:	2 minute, 30 seconds

Overview: Bruce delivers a rote prayer for world peace. God challenges him to pray for what he really cares about. Bruce sincerely asks that Grace would meet someone who would love her completely—someone who would have God's "eyesight" when he looks at her. God proclaims his second prayer "good."

Illustration: Jesus taught the disciples to pray, so do the same for your students. Discourage posturing before God trying to sound high, mighty, and spiritual. Instead, model how to lay a heart and soul bare, bringing before the loving Father our deepest needs, fears, dreams, and requests.

Questions:
• What are the ingredients for a prayer that pleases God?
• Read Matthew 6:5-15. **Does Jesus mean that you're supposed to quote this prayer every day? Why or why not?**
• **Why does God want us to pray if he already knows everything?**
• **When have you seen prayer directly affect a situation?**
• **What stops you from praying more often?**

Prayer Requests | I WANT A LAMBORGHINI

	Title: **ARMAGEDDON**	
HUMOR	Touchstone Pictures, 1998	**PG-13**

Scripture: John 15:5-8
Alternate Take: Helping Others (Matthew 25:32-46)

DVD CHAPTER:	5
START TIME:	33 minutes, 45 seconds
START CUE:	Stamper approaches.

END TIME:	35 minutes, 30 seconds
END CUE:	Stamper says, "None of them want to pay taxes again. Ever."
DURATION:	1 minute, 45 seconds

Overview: Stamper reads off the list of demands from the crew. The government agrees to honor every one of the team's strange requests, and the team agrees to take the job.

Illustration: God promises to answer all of our prayers, but you don't see everyone in the world kicking it beach side with the bold and beautiful. Bring some context to Christ's promise, helping your students learn how to send God the requests that he will honor.

Questions:

- **What is the strangest request you or someone you know has brought to God? What happened?**
- Read John 15:5-8. **Does Jesus fulfill his promise to answer whatever we wish? Why or why not?**
- **What does it mean to "remain" in Christ?**
- **How does connecting more closely with Christ transform our prayer requests?**
- **What do you earnestly seek from God in prayer? How might you need to change your request in light of these verses?**

Predestination | WHAT WILL YOU DO?

Title: **MINORITY REPORT**		
DRAMA	20th Century Fox, 2002	**PG-13**

Scripture: Joshua 24:14-15

Alternate Take: Choices (Proverbs 1:28-33)

DVD CHAPTER:	22
START TIME:	2 hours, 12 minutes, 45 seconds
START CUE:	Agatha flops in the water.
END TIME:	2 hours, 14 minutes, 45 seconds
END CUE:	Lamar says, "Forgive me, John."
DURATION:	2 minutes

Overview: The Precogs predict Lamar will murder John, and Lamar must choose whether to ruin Precrime by not killing John or prove the system right by committing the murder. John claims that seeing the future affords Lamar the opportunity to change it. What will Lamar choose?

Illustration: The Bible speaks of both predestination and free will, so we must wrestle with the truth that lies between. While God has laid out our very steps before us, we aren't marionettes forced to walk in robotic lockstep. Help your teenagers take comfort in God's plan for their lives while making smart choices in getting there.

Questions:

- **Do you believe in predestination? Explain.**
- **Why does the thought of predestination frustrate many people?**

- Read Joshua 24:14-15. **How can predestination and free will coexist?**
- **Why bother making plans and choices if God has predestined them?**
- **How can some form of predestination be a source of comfort?**

Prejudice | I'LL DO IT MY WAY

Title: JONAH: A VEGGIETALES MOVIE	
HUMOR Artisan, 2002	G

Scripture: Colossians 3:11

Alternate Takes: Consequences (Psalm 75:6-7), Jonah (Jonah 1:1-3)

DVD CHAPTER:	11
START TIME:	34 minutes, 45 seconds
START CUE:	The captain says, "OK, here's the deal."
END TIME:	37 minutes, 00 seconds
END CUE:	Gold Tooth says, "Oooo. Fish slappers."
DURATION:	2 minutes, 15 seconds

Overview: Everyone plays Go Fish. The person with the last card is the one who caused the storm. Jonah gets the last card and admits he's running from God. That's why the storm hit. He just doesn't like those nasty people from Nineveh!

Illustration: It's completely illogical to hold animosity toward a group of people based on skin color, geographic location, social class, music preference—you name it—but we do it all the time. Challenge any prejudices within your ministry, making it clear God accepts any and all into his family and we must do the same.

Questions:
- **How have you seen prejudice bring harm to people?**
- **What beliefs or attitudes fuel prejudice?**
- Read Colossians 3:11. **Why is prejudice especially out of place in the church?**
- **How does prejudice strike at the very heart of the good news message?**
- **How can you fight prejudicial attitudes in your own life?**

Preparation | GOT YOUR HELMET?

Title: FRIDAY NIGHT LIGHTS	
DRAMA Universal Pictures, 2004	PG–13

Scripture: Matthew 25:1-13

Alternate Take: Armor of God (Ephesians 6:11-17)

DVD CHAPTER:	9
START TIME:	29 minutes, 45 seconds
START CUE:	Gaines says, "Comer! You're in the game."
END TIME:	30 minutes, 30 seconds

END CUE:	Comer is told to sit back down.
DURATION:	45 seconds

Overview: Coach Gaines puts Comer in the game. The boy runs for the field, but Coach grabs him, and asks, "Where's your helmet?" Comer can't find it, so he misses his opportunity to play.

Illustration: All of those Christians out there saying they'll become moral when they're older or really get serious about faith down the road just don't get it. We must be prepared to jump in the game at a moment's notice. Challenge your ministry to get their game on and prepare now for any unexpected call.

Questions:
- What happened the last time you weren't prepared for something?
- What excuses do we give for not preparing for things we know are coming?
- Read Matthew 25:1-13. What spiritual things does God want us prepared for at all times?
- How does a person go about preparing for these things?
- What must you do to become better prepared?

Pride | I'M THE STAR!

Title: **ALONG CAME POLLY**		
HUMOR	Universal Pictures, 2004	PG-13

Scripture: Proverbs 11:2
Alternate Take: Selfishness (Philippians 2:3-8)

DVD CHAPTER:	7
START TIME:	29 minutes, 00 seconds
START CUE:	An outside shot of Hell's Kitchen Community Center is shown on the screen.
END TIME:	30 minutes, 00 seconds
END CUE:	Sandy says, "Whatever, Reuben."
DURATION:	1 minute

Overview: Reuben watches Sandy rehearse *Jesus Christ Superstar*. Sandy takes Jesus' solo, singing and dancing out of turn. The actor portraying Jesus complains, but Sandy says he's the star and will do whatever he wants.

Illustration: It's so stupid to brag about our talents and abilities because God is the one who gives these gifts in the first place. This scene shows how ridiculous pride in one's abilities can be. Help your youth learn what humility and proper pride look like in their lives.

Questions:
- What is the most prideful thing you've ever seen someone do?
- Why do people hate prideful behavior?
- Read Proverbs 11:2. Does this mean we can't be proud of our abilities? Explain.

- What makes pride so destructive to our friendships? to our relationship with God?
- How can you become humble in an area where you struggle with pride?

Priorities | WHAT'S MORE IMPORTANT?

DRAMA	Title: **DADDY DAY CARE**	**PG**
	Columbia Pictures, 2003	

Scripture: Matthew 6:9-13

Alternate Takes: Family (1 Timothy 5:8), Materialism (1 Timothy 6:9-11), Success (2 Chronicles 25:19-22)

DVD CHAPTER:	24
START TIME:	1 hour, 16 minutes, 45 seconds
START CUE:	Marvin says, "Now wait a minute."
END TIME:	1 hour, 30 minutes, 00 seconds
END CUE:	Charlie says, "I wish it was that simple."
DURATION:	2 minutes, 30 seconds

Overview: Marvin is upset that Charlie and Phil are ditching Daddy Day Care for jobs with big salaries and prestige. They want Marvin to join them, but he refuses—he insists they're doing something important with the kids! Charlie tries to explain to his son why he's quitting, and the child offers to sell all his toys so his dad can stay.

Illustration: Everyone knows it's supposed to be "God, Family, Self" on the priority list, but things tend to get jumbled or replaced with other things much less worthy. Encourage your teenagers to set their priorities now so they can remain focused and balanced as the demands on their lives begin to pile up.

Questions:
- What do people typically list as priorities in life?
- Do you think our society puts the most value on what we claim as priorities? Why or why not?
- Read Matthew 6:9-13. What surprises you about Jesus' list of priorities?
- How might making these things your priorities in life radically change your focus?
- What priorities do you need to shift, and how will you do that?

Put-Downs | WELL, YOU'RE A STUPID HEAD

HUMOR	Title: **LEGALLY BLONDE 2: RED, WHITE & BLONDE**	**PG-13**
	MGM, 2003	

Scripture: Ephesians 4:29-32

Alternate Takes: Encouragement (1 Thessalonians 5:11), Taming the Tongue (James 3:5-10)

Themes **P-R**

DVD CHAPTER:	10
START TIME:	23 minutes, 00 seconds
START CUE:	Grace and Timothy argue.
END TIME:	25 minutes, 15 seconds
END CUE:	Elle says, "I think the snap cup really works."
DURATION:	2 minutes, 15 seconds

Overview: Grace and Timothy argue until Elle sings the "snap cup" song. She tells everyone to write a compliment about a co-worker and put it in the cup. Elle will read the notes, and everyone will be encouraged. After an initial compliment for Grace, Elle reads one that says she's stupid.

Illustration: It's so easy to cut people with our words. Even though it's often done in the name of good fun, these jokes can still hurt. Try to create a "no put-down" zone within your ministry so your students see how encouraging life can be without sharpened tongues.

Questions:
- Why do put-downs hurt so much?
- Why do people continue to put down others even if they know it hurts?
- Read Ephesians 4:29-32. How hard is it for you to obey these verses?
- How can you work on erasing all the put-downs from your vocabulary?

Rejection | GET OUT OF MY HOUSE!

	Title: **DIARY OF A MAD BLACK WOMAN**	
DRAMA	Lions Gate Films, 2005	**PG-13**

Scripture: 2 Corinthians 1:3-7
Alternate Takes: Adultery (Proverbs 6:32-35), Divorce (Matthew 19:3-8)

DVD CHAPTER:	2
START TIME:	9 minutes, 45 seconds
START CUE:	Brenda enters the house.
END TIME:	12 minutes, 15 seconds
END CUE:	Charles slams the door.
DURATION:	2 minutes, 30 seconds

Overview: Charles informs Helen that their 18-year marriage is over. He's kicking her out and having his girlfriend Brenda and the two kids they have together move in. Helen refuses to leave, so Charles drags her out of the house and locks the door.

Illustration: Rejection feels awful. Though we probably won't be rebuffed quite so dramatically as this, the emotions can be just as intense. Help your young people find peace and healing in Jesus when others reject them.

Questions:
- How does this scene capture the emotional anguish of rejection?

- How do you typically cope with rejection?
- Read 2 Corinthians 1:3-7. **Do you find Jesus to be a good comfort in times of rejection? Why or why not?**
- What promises does God give us that can provide stability during a time of rejection?
- How can we help one another draw strength from God during times of rejection?

Relevance | JESUS IS MY HOMEBOY

Title:	BRINGING DOWN THE HOUSE	PG-13
HUMOR	Touchstone Pictures, 2003	

Scripture: 1 Corinthians 9:19-23
Alternate Take: Christianese (1 Corinthians 14:6-11)

DVD CHAPTER:	2
START TIME:	14 minutes, 30 seconds
START CUE:	Peter says, "Where exactly have you been?"
END TIME:	15 minutes, 00 seconds
END CUE:	Charlene says, "Don't you hear good?"
DURATION:	30 seconds

Overview: Charlene explains what happened in ghetto-speak. Peter has no idea what she is saying.

Illustration: How "cool" do we need to try and make Jesus in order to make him acceptable to the mainstream? Discuss what the non-negotiables are concerning Christ, faith, and church, and then uncover ways to make those eternal truths connect with modern audiences in relevant ways.

Questions:
- **What do people need to do in order to be effectively relevant to their audience?**
- Read 1 Corinthians 9:19-23. **How do these verses illustrate the need to make the gospel relevant?**
- **What are the "non-negotiables" in our faith that never change in relation to relevance?**
- **How can we make the timeless message of the gospel in our ministry more relevant to your friends?**

Repentance | FLIP A U-TURN

Title:	JONAH: A VEGGIETALES MOVIE	G
HUMOR	Artisan, 2002	

Scripture: 2 Corinthians 7:8-10
Alternate Takes: Confrontation (Luke 17:3), Mercy (Ephesians 2:4-7)

Themes **P-R**

DVD CHAPTER:	19
START TIME:	1 hour, 2 minutes, 30 seconds
START CUE:	The guard says, "What did you say?"
END TIME:	1 hour, 5 minutes, 00 seconds
END CUE:	The king proclaims, "Let Asparagus and his friends go free."
DURATION:	2 minutes, 30 seconds

Overview: Jonah claims he was in the belly of a whale, got spit out, and came to give them the message: "Stop it!" He warns them that if they don't change, the city will be destroyed. The king commands the people to repent because God might give them a second chance.

Illustration: Repentance is that simple—stop it! God wants us to simply cease and desist our sinful ways and turn around toward him. Encourage your young people to follow the king's advice and take the opportunity to repent now.

Questions:
- **What are some reactions people have when confronted with their sin?**
- **What makes repentance difficult, even when you know you're wrong?**
- Read 2 Corinthians 7:8-10. **What ingredients go into genuine repentance?**
- **Why does God seek repentance rather than simply making people stop doing bad things?**
- **Is there anything you need to repent of right now? If so, what's stopping you?**

Reputation | AN EASY THING TO LOSE

HUMOR	Title: **WIN A DATE WITH TAD HAMILTON!** DreamWorks, 2004	**PG-13**

Scripture: Proverbs 22:1
Alternate Takes: Facades (Acts 5:1-11), Image (2 Samuel 15:1-6)

DVD CHAPTER:	1
START TIME:	2 minutes, 15 seconds
START CUE:	Tad exits his car.
END TIME:	4 minutes, 30 seconds
END CUE:	Tad screams, "Wow!"
DURATION:	2 minutes, 15 seconds

Overview: Pete, Rosie, and Cathy watch Tad Hamilton's war movie. The girls think Tad's wonderful and probably exactly like the characters he plays; however, he is actually drinking and driving at that moment.

Illustration: A reputation takes a lifetime to build and only a moment to lose. Discover what kinds of reputations the kids in your ministry are building, how they can be modified in more Christ-like directions if necessary, and practical ways for protecting them.

Questions:
- Is it fair that a person's reputation can be destroyed with one stupid action? Why or why not?
- Read Proverbs 22:1. **How does a person build up his or her good name?**
- What effect does a person's reputation have on Jesus, both positive and negative?
- What can you do to build and protect a reputation that glorifies God?

Respect | HE'S STILL THE KING

DRAMA	Title: **HERO**	
	Miramax Films, 2004	PG-13

Scripture: 1 Samuel 24:1-12
Alternate Takes: Authority (Romans 13:1-4)

DVD CHAPTER:	9
START TIME:	59 minutes, 15 seconds
START CUE:	A close-up of Broken Sword's face is shown on the screen.
END TIME:	1 hour, 2 minutes, 00 seconds
END CUE:	Nameless salutes Snow.
DURATION:	2 minutes, 45 seconds

Overview: Nameless proves that he can kill the king with deadly accuracy. He needs Broken Sword's and Snow's help in getting close to him. Snow says they wouldn't have to if Broken Sword had killed the king when he had the chance. Broken Sword proclaims he will protect the king.

Illustration: God calls us to respect all people, even those we disagree with or possibly even hate. Help your youth understand what this means and how they can show it to others.

Questions:
- Read 1 Samuel 24:1-12. **Was David foolish to respect Saul? Why or why not?**
- **How do we show someone respect, even when he or she is wrong?**
- **Why does God allow disreputable people to attain positions of power?**
- **How does showing respect to all human beings, no matter their position, honor God?**
- **Do you need to show more respect to someone? If so, how will you do that?**

Responsibility | THE "NOT ME" DID IT

HUMOR	Title: **HOLES**	
	Walt Disney Pictures, 2003	PG

Scripture: Genesis 3:8-13
Alternate Take: Blame (Numbers 20:2-5)

Themes P-R

DVD CHAPTER:	10
START TIME:	33 minutes, 30 seconds
START CUE:	The exterior of the sleeping quarters is shown on the screen.
END TIME:	34 minutes, 30 seconds
END CUE:	Pendanski points to his head.
DURATION:	1 minute

Overview: All of the guys blame their sentence to Camp Green Lake on other people or on random circumstances. Pendanski assures them that their own mistakes landed them there. They each have but one life, and they're screwing it up.

Illustration: Nobody wants to take responsibility for mistakes. In fact, people would rather sue others than admit ignorance. But God calls his followers to take a higher path, accepting responsibility and finding freedom in his grace.

Questions:
- **What is the lamest excuse you've heard from someone ducking responsibility?**
- Read Genesis 3:8-13. **Why do we naturally shift responsibility, even when it's obviously our fault?**
- **How does taking responsibility for our actions cause faith to grow? build a positive reputation? honor God?**
- **What must you do in order to become willing to accept responsibility for your actions?**

Righteous Anger | I WON'T STAND FOR IT!

	Title: **NICHOLAS NICKLEBY**	
DRAMA	MGM, 2002	PG

Scripture: John 2:13-17
Alternate Takes: Injustice (Isaiah 59:14-20), Pity (Proverbs 14:21)

DVD CHAPTER:	10
START TIME:	35 minutes, 45 seconds
START CUE:	All the boys stand at attention.
END TIME:	38 minutes, 00 seconds
END CUE:	Nicholas and Smike exit.
DURATION:	2 minutes, 15 seconds

Overview: Squeers prepares to cane Smike when Nicholas jumps to Smike's defense. He warns Squeers not to touch the innocent young man and backs up his words by wresting the cane from the wretched man and beating him with it. Nicholas stops, saying Squeers is receiving the pity he never extended the children.

Illustration: It's not only acceptable, but it is our duty to allow righteous anger to fuel acts of courage and justice. Help your students discern between Christ-like and ungodly anger, and help them channel this fiery passion in the proper direction.

- Do you think Nicholas was justified in his actions? Why or why not?
- When was the last time you were filled with anger over an injustice? What did you do?
- Read John 2:13-17. How does Jesus' action line up with his reputation as the sinless, loving, merciful Son of God?
- What is the difference between anger and righteous anger?
- How must Christians respond when righteous anger fills them?

Risk | THERE'S ALWAYS SOME

Title: **LADDER 49**	
DRAMA Touchstone Pictures, 2004	PG-13

Scripture: 1 Samuel 14:1-14

Alternate Takes: Helping Others (Proverbs 14:31), Sacrifice (Romans 5:7)

DVD CHAPTER:	9
START TIME:	1 hour, 14 minutes, 45 seconds
START CUE:	Nick says, Hey, dad?"
END TIME:	1 hour, 16 minutes, 30 seconds
END CUE:	Jack says, "Can you do that for me?"
DURATION:	1 minute, 45 seconds

Overview: Nick asks if steam can melt your face. Jack admits steam burns, but skin grows back. Nick doesn't want his dad to get hurt. Jack says he's trained not to get hurt, but things go wrong sometimes. He does what's necessary to save lives.

Illustration: American Christianity seems to believe God wants us to live in safe little cocoons, but the Bible is full of men and women who took great risks, stepping out in faith to follow God's call on their lives. Challenge your teenagers to take the risks God asks of them, trusting in his divine plan for their lives.

Questions:
- Does God promise that we will always be protected and safe? Explain.
- Why is risk essential for growth as both people and children of God?
- Read 1 Samuel 14:1-14. How does a person know when God wants them to take a "crazy" risk?
- Why can Christians take radical risks without fear?
- Where do you feel God calling you to take a risk and how will you do that?

P-R

Themes

Sacrifice | GO ON WITHOUT ME

	Title: **ARMAGEDDON**	
DRAMA	Touchstone Pictures, 1998	**PG-13**

Scripture: Philippians 2:14-17
Alternate Take: Duty (Matthew 22:37-40)

DVD CHAPTER:	24
START TIME:	2 hours, 9 minutes, 15 seconds
START CUE:	Harry holds up the straws.
END TIME:	2 hours, 11 minutes, 30 seconds
END CUE:	Stamper says, "That's your job."
DURATION:	2 minutes, 15 seconds

Overview: Rescue team members draw straws to determine who must sacrifice his life to save the world. A.J. draws the short straw. Stamper takes him down to the asteroid surface and yanks out A.J.'s oxygen hose. As A.J. is unable to continue, Stamper takes his place, sacrificing himself so A.J. might live.

Illustration: A self-centered world finds sacrifice to be a foreign concept. That's what makes Jesus' action on the cross so powerful—the sinless creator dying out of selfless love for his sin-plagued creation. As followers of Christ, we must emulate him with small sacrificial choices that make a huge impact on those we serve while knitting our souls to the Savior.

Questions:
- **Would you take someone's place on a suicide mission as Stamper did? Why or why not?**
- **Do people who sacrifice for others receive respect and recognition? Explain.**
- Read Philippians 2:14-17. **Does being "poured out" require a person to lose his or her life? Explain.**
- **How does our personal sacrifice point others to Jesus?**
- **What are some practical, everyday ways a person can make sacrifices for other people?**

Salvation | WHAT'S THE FINE PRINT?

	Title: **THE SANTA CLAUSE 2**	
HUMOR	Walt Disney Pictures, 2002	**G**

Scripture: Romans 10:8-13
Alternate Take: Assurance (Romans 8:35-39)

DVD CHAPTER:	4
START TIME:	14 minutes, 45 seconds
START CUE:	Curtis rolls in a magnifying glass.

END TIME:	17 minutes, 45 seconds
END CUE:	"Christmas is getting very complicated."
DURATION:	3 minutes

Overview: Curtis tells Santa there's a second clause. In ultra-fine print, it says he must get married. If he doesn't fulfill the "Mrs. Clause" in 28 days, he goes through "de-Santafication."

Illustration: Praise God there's no fine print when it comes to saving faith in his Son. Explain the big picture on salvation while giving your youth assurance there won't be a hidden clause that can take it away once received.

Questions:

- **Do you ever fear there is a hidden clause you've missed concerning salvation? Explain.**
- Read Romans 10:8-13. **What is the recipe in these verses for salvation?**
- **How can a person be sure that they genuinely confess and believe?**
- **Why might someone refuse the free gift of salvation?**
- **What are some changes you will see in the life of a person who is saved?**

Satan | HE'S RAVENOUS

Title: **RABBIT-PROOF FENCE**

DRAMA   Miramax Films, 2002   PG

Scripture: 1 Peter 5:8-10
Alternate Take: Tragedy (Isaiah 22:3-4)

DVD CHAPTER:	3
START TIME:	8 minutes, 45 seconds
START CUE:	Women are shopping.
END TIME:	11 minutes, 45 seconds
END CUE:	A woman hits her head with a rock.
DURATION:	3 minutes

Overview: Molly's mom says Mr. Neville can't take her daughters. Police arrive, and mothers tell their daughters to run. The cops catch the girls, drag them into the car, and drive away.

Illustration: The devil knows where he's headed in the end, and he wants to take as many of us there with him as possible. Use this gripping scene to illustrate his passion for stealing souls for himself or derailing Christians from making a difference for the kingdom of God. Give your students some practical defenses against him.

Questions:

- **How does this scene illustrate what the devil wants to do?**
- **What are some characteristics of Satan?**
- **What evidence do you see or not see of Satan's activity on earth?**

- Read 1 Peter 5:8-10. **Why can't the devil drag us away?**
- **What changes should you make in your spiritual life that take you and others into account Satan's desire to tempt and drag away?**

Second Chances | I DON'T KNOW HIM!

| **DRAMA** | Title: **THE PASSION OF THE CHRIST** | R |
| | New Market Films, 2004 | |

Scripture: John 21:10-19

Alternate Takes: Denying Christ (Matthew 26:30-35), Shame (Ezra 9:5-9)

DVD CHAPTER:	9
START TIME:	29 minutes, 00 seconds
START CUE:	The Pharisees exit the temple.
END TIME:	31 minutes, 45 seconds
END CUE:	Peter runs away from Mary.
DURATION:	2 minutes, 45 seconds

Overview: Peter watches Jesus being beaten. When a man identifies Peter as one of Jesus' followers, Peter denies the charge. Struggling to flee, he is recognized twice more. Peter adamantly denies his association with Jesus…then the cock crows. He locks eyes with his Master…and he remembers Jesus' prophecy.

Illustration: This scene only begins to capture the tremendous devastation Peter, whom Jesus called the rock, must have felt at that moment. Encourage your students by pointing them to the rest of the story. Jesus welcomes his disciple and builds his church upon this "weakling's" back! Won't he offer every young person a second chance as well?

Questions:
- **Could you ever forgive a friend who turned his or her back on you like that? Why or why not?**
- **What are some "modern" ways people turn their backs on Jesus today?**
- Read John 21:10-19. **What feelings must have been running through Peter when he saw Jesus?**
- **Why does God use mess-ups and failures to do great things in his kingdom, such as building the church?**
- **Will Jesus refuse to give anyone a second chance who asks? Why or why not?**

Secrets | THEY ALWAYS CATCH UP

| **HUMOR** | Title: **OCEAN'S 12** | PG-13 |
| | Warner Brothers, 2004 | |

Scripture: Jeremiah 23:23-24

Alternate Take: Grace (Hebrews 4:13-16)

DVD CHAPTER:	1
START TIME:	1 minute, 00 seconds
START CUE:	Rusty walks to Isabel in bed.
END TIME:	2 minutes, 30 seconds
END CUE:	Rusty jumps out the window.
DURATION:	1 minute, 30 seconds

Overview: Isabel says she's got a break in the burglary case she's working on, a boot print and hair—both of which will name Rusty the culprit. Knowing he'll be busted, Rusty jumps out the window.

Illustration: Secrets always catch up with you. That's why it's best to come clean at the beginning. Help your young people see the long-term damage caused by secrets now so they don't have to jump out any future windows.

Questions:
- Why do our secrets tend to always find their way into the light?
- Read Jeremiah 23:23-24. **What reasons do we have for keeping secrets despite this fact?**
- How do secrets weigh on a person's relationships? on his or her connection with God?
- Is there a secret you need to confess? If so, what's stopping you?

Self-Control | YOU CAN'T MAKE ME

DRAMA	Title: **HULK**	PG-13
	Universal Pictures, 2003	

Scripture: Titus 2:11-14
Alternate Take: Peacemaker (Matthew 5:38-48)

DVD CHAPTER:	20
START TIME:	1 hour, 24 minutes, 45 seconds
START CUE:	Bruce washes his face.
END TIME:	1 hour, 26 minutes, 30 seconds
END CUE:	Talbot says, "Subconsciously, I bet that's another story."
DURATION:	1 minute, 45 seconds

Overview: Talbot asks Bruce if he can take some cells from his body while he's the Hulk. Bruce refuses, so Talbot shocks him repeatedly with a TASER. Bruce controls his anger, so Talbot knocks him unconscious.

Illustration: Boy, Bruce shows some big-league self-control in this scene. Too bad the same can't be said of the road-ragers, angry parents at sporting events, and illegal downloaders! Challenge your teens to bring back the forgotten art of self-control to our instant-gratification society.

Questions:

- Would you be able to exhibit Bruce's level of self-control? Why or why not?
- How have you or someone you know gotten into trouble for lack of self-control?
- Read Titus 2:11-14. What does a life of self-control look like in everyday life?
- How does a person know when to practice self-control and when to act?
- Where do you need to practice more self-control, and how will you learn to do that?

Self-Esteem | IT'S HOW YOU PLAY THE GAME

HUMOR	Title: **MEET THE FOCKERS**	PG-13
	Universal Pictures, 2004	

Scripture: Psalm 139:13-16

Alternate Take: Competition (1 Corinthians 9:24-27)

DVD CHAPTER:	5
START TIME:	27 minutes, 30 seconds
START CUE:	Bernie turns on the lights.
END TIME:	28 minutes, 30 seconds
END CUE:	Bernie says, "Well, whatever works."
DURATION:	1 minute

Overview: Bernie shows the "Wall of Gaylord," which holds all of Greg's childhood awards, such as ninth-place ribbons. Bernie wanted to instill great worth in his son, not concern for winning. Jack disagrees, claiming competition is essential.

Illustration: What does it take to build healthy self-esteem, and how does that self-image play into our spiritual life? Explore these questions with your students, helping them find their worth in Christ rather than in any ribbons and trophies.

Questions:

- Have your parents done a good job building your self-esteem? Why or why not?
- What ingredients go into building a person's self-esteem?
- Read Psalm 139:13-14. Why is this passage the perfect foundation for someone's self-esteem?
- How does our self-esteem affect our relationship with others? with God?
- How can you rely more heavily on God to strengthen your self-esteem?

Selfishness | ME, MYSELF, AND I

DRAMA	Title: **ABOUT A BOY**	PG-13
	Universal Pictures, 2002	

Scripture: 1 Peter 4:8-10

Alternate Take: Compassion (1 Peter 3:8)

DVD CHAPTER:	7
START TIME:	25 minutes, 45 seconds
START CUE:	A car pulls up.
END TIME:	26 minutes, 45 seconds
END CUE:	The car drives away.
DURATION:	1 minute

Overview: Will drops off Marcus after Marcus' mother attempts suicide. Will shows absolutely no compassion for the hurting boy because Will is the star of his own TV show. People come in and out of his show, some remaining longer than others, but ultimately they all depart, allowing him to remain the center of his universe.

Illustration: Though few of your youth would be so callous, Will's words ring uncomfortably true. Selfishness comes hardwired into our bones, and it's only through God's grace we can focus on the needs of others. Identify selfish areas and how it affects our choices and relationships.

Questions:
- **What motivates selfishness?**
- **What situations tend to bring out your own selfishness?**
- Read 1 Peter 4:8-10. **How does following these verses kill selfishness?**
- **Where is the line between selfishness and simply looking out for your own needs?**
- **What selfish attitudes do you need to change and how will you do that?**

Sensitivity | I CAN'T BELIEVE YOU SAID THAT

HUMOR	Title: **DODGEBALL: A TRUE UNDERDOG STORY**	PG-13
	20th Century Fox, 2004	

Scripture: 1 Samuel 1:9-17
Alternate Take: Body Image (1 Peter 3:3-4)

DVD CHAPTER:	1
START TIME:	45 seconds
START CUE:	White says, "I'm White Goodman."
END TIME:	1 minute, 45 seconds
END CUE:	A picture labeled "White Goodman 1987" is shown on the screen.
DURATION:	1 minute

Overview: White promotes Globo Gym, guaranteeing that its weight training and cosmetic surgery services will transform ugly, fat people into beautiful beings. He claims staying "repulsive" is each person's own fault.

Illustration: This clip is incredibly insensitive, and opens up a great discussion on how Christians must build an important filter of sensitivity into their lives. Offhand remarks and actions can cut to a person's core, so help your youth find ways to become sensitive to the needs and feelings of others.

Questions:

- What is the most insensitive thing you've heard someone say?
- What attitudes or traits do insensitive people share?
- Read 1 Samuel 1:9-17. **How might Samuel have been more sensitive to Hannah's plight?**
- Why is it so important for Christians and the church to become sensitive to others?
- How can we become more sensitive as a church family to the needs of others?

Serving Others | IT'S OUR DUTY

Title: FIRST KNIGHT	
DRAMA Columbia Pictures, 1995	**PG-13**

Scripture: John 13:3-16
Alternate Take: Equality (Proverbs 22:2)

DVD CHAPTER:	17
START TIME:	46 minutes, 00 seconds
START CUE:	Arthur says, "Come."
END TIME:	47 minutes, 15 seconds
END CUE:	Arthur sheathes his sword.
DURATION:	1 minute, 15 seconds

Overview: Arthur explains to Lancelot his philosophy of treating every person as worthy and equal—that's why the table is round. He believes death is meaningful when it comes in serving someone else. He believes that "in serving each other, we become free."

Illustration: Jesus gave the same call to his "knights" 2,000 years ago—to serve any and all in humility. It's a bizarre truth of God's kingdom that the servants find freedom and honor. Hold up the behavior Jesus modeled, encouraging everyone in your ministry to emulate him by sitting at his "round table."

Questions:

- Why don't people naturally set up "round tables" in our society?
- Read John 13:3-16. **What makes Jesus' teaching here so radical?**
- What are some reasons people, even Christians, have for not obeying Jesus' command?
- How would our world change for the better if everyone put this teaching into practice?
- What must you do in your own life to put his teaching into practice?

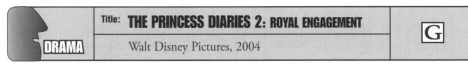

Title: THE PRINCESS DIARIES 2: ROYAL ENGAGEMENT	
DRAMA	Walt Disney Pictures, 2004	G

Scripture: Deuteronomy 22:13-21

Alternate Take: Sexism (Genesis 1:27)

DVD CHAPTER:	11
START TIME:	1 hour, 33 minutes, 45 seconds
START CUE:	Mia approaches the podium.
END TIME:	1 hour, 35 minutes, 30 seconds
END CUE:	The crowd claps.
DURATION:	1 minute, 45 seconds

Overview: Mia admits to the wedding guests that she was only getting married because of the law. However, her grandmother ruled well for years without a husband. So she asks the members of parliament to think about their sisters, wives, and daughters. Would they ask of them what they're asking of her? She's prepared to rule, but not with a husband at this time.

Illustration: This is a great clip to show your young men before asking them: Would you want your mother, sister, or daughter to have premarital sex? It's a probing question, and it may help them see each young woman as another's loved one and not a potential sack mate. Challenge them to reserve sex for the marriage bed.

Questions:
- Would you want your sister or your future wife engaging in premarital sex? Why or why not?
- Read Deuteronomy 22:13-21. **Why did they take premarital sex so seriously in the Old Testament?**
- Why does there seem to be a double standard between men and women in regards to premarital sex, both in the verses and today?
- How does saving sex for marriage protect a person physically and spiritually?
- What must you do to protect yourself from engaging in premarital sex?

Sexual Boundaries | HANDS OFF

Title: X2: X-MEN UNITED	
DRAMA	20th Century Fox, 2003	PG-13

Scripture: Song of Songs 3:1-5

Alternate Take: Temptation (Genesis 39:5-12)

DVD CHAPTER:	18
START TIME:	51 minutes, 45 seconds
START CUE:	Rogue puts her hand on Iceman's shoulder.

Themes

S-Z

END TIME:	52 minutes, 15 seconds
END CUE:	Iceman says, "It's OK."
DURATION:	30 seconds

Overview: Rogue and Bobby kiss briefly, and nothing bad happens. They kiss more passionately, and Rogue starts sucking the power and life out of Bobby. He shoves her away seconds before permanent damage occurs.

Illustration: Kissing won't steal your life force, but sexual intimacy outside of marriage can hold grave consequences. God pronounced sex "good"…within certain boundaries. Encourage your young people to set boundaries now before they make poor choices while caught in the heat of passion.

Questions:
- Have you created sexual boundaries for yourself? Why or why not?
- Why did God place boundaries on sex?
- Read Song of Songs 3:1-5. **What is so dangerous about arousing passion?**
- What benefits come from maintaining your sexual boundaries?
- What situations tempt you to cross your boundaries, and how can you stop yourself from doing so?

Sexual Intimacy | YOU CAN'T FORGET

DRAMA	Title: **50 FIRST DATES**	PG-13
	Columbia Pictures, 2004	

Scripture: 1 Corinthians 6:15-20
Alternate Takes: Jesus' Love (Romans 8:35-39), Regret (Proverbs 5:11-13)

DVD CHAPTER:	16
START TIME:	1 hour, 14 minutes, 30 seconds
START CUE:	Lucy says, "Henry?"
END TIME:	1 hour, 16 minutes, 45 seconds
END CUE:	Lucy leaves.
DURATION:	2 minutes, 15 seconds

Overview: Lucy tells Henry she's breaking up with him. She doesn't want him throwing his life and career away for her happiness. She plans to erase him completely from her life by tearing the pages about him out of her journal, that way she won't remember.

Illustration: It sure would be nice if we could forget our sexual partners this easily, but it's impossible. Sexual intimacy at any level creates a bond with the other person. That's why it's imperative to save as much as possible for your spouse, so you (and your spouse) don't have to deal with the lingering memories of your sexual past.

Questions:

- Is there anyone you've dated that you'd like to erase from your memory? If so, why?
- Read 1 Corinthians 6:15-20. **What makes it impossible to erase the memory of someone we've been sexually intimate with?**
- Is sex the only act of physical intimacy that leaves a lasting bond? Why or why not?
- How can you protect yourself from becoming sexually intimate with someone?
- How can God help people dissolve any sexual connections they've made with others?

Sexual Purity | YOU CAN ONLY GIVE IT AWAY ONCE

HUMOR	Title: **WIN A DATE WITH TAD HAMILTON!**	**PG-13**
	DreamWorks, 2004	

Scripture: 1 Peter 2:9-11
Alternate Take: Boundaries (Song of Songs 3:1-5)

DVD CHAPTER:	16
START TIME:	52 minutes, 45 seconds
START CUE:	A Piggly Wiggly scanner display is shown on the screen.
END TIME:	54 minutes, 00 seconds
END CUE:	The priest chuckles.
DURATION:	1 minute, 15 seconds

Overview: Pete grills Rosie about whether she got physical with Tad. She claims Tad didn't want to harm their friendship. Pete mocks her gullibility, saying every guy uses that line to get a girl—even a nearby priest admits to using it.

Illustration: It's time to get brutally honest with the ladies in your ministry about male intentions—they ain't pure. Challenge both the men and the women to cherish their purity. It's a gift that can be bestowed once and only once, so don't toss it away like a fool.

Questions:

- Is Pete right? Why or why not?
- Why are some people willing to say or do anything to steal another's purity?
- Read 1 Peter 2:9-11. **How is sexual temptation waging war against our souls?**
- What must a person do to fight and protect his or her purity?
- What spiritual benefits come from remaining pure? What social benefits?

S-Z

Themes

Sharing Faith | WOULD YOU BELIEVE...?

HUMOR

Title: MEN IN BLACK II

Columbia Pictures, 2002

PG-13

Scripture: Luke 24:44-53
Alternate Take: Belief (Acts 13:40-41)

DVD CHAPTER:	7
START TIME:	21 minutes, 45 seconds
START CUE:	The screen shows the exterior of a diner.
END TIME:	22 minutes, 45 seconds
END CUE:	Jay says, "OK."
DURATION:	1 minute

Overview: Laura claims to be OK despite witnessing aliens murder a man she's known her whole life. She believes there are more aliens out there and simply wants to know what to believe. Agent Jay tells her the truth about his organization's dealings with alien life, and she accepts it.

Illustration: Talking about faith in God can feel similar to expounding on the existence of aliens. Nevertheless, Jesus calls us to proclaim his name, share his story, and follow his teachings while on earth no matter how people might react. Remind your youth that doing so might be frightening, but others' ability to accept the "fantastic" truth might surprise them.

Questions:

- **Does talking about God ever seem as crazy as talking about aliens? Why or why not?**
- **How have you seen people react to the message of Jesus? If it's the truth, why do people have different reactions?**
- Read Luke 24:44-53. **What's your responsibility in sharing your faith with others?**
- **When is it appropriate to share your faith? When is it inappropriate?**
- **Whom would you like to share your faith with and how will you do that?**

Signs | GIVE ME ONE, GOD!

HUMOR

Title: BRUCE ALMIGHTY

Universal Pictures, 2003

PG-13

Scripture: Mark 8:1-13
Alternate Take: Prayer (Proverbs 15:29)

DVD CHAPTER:	5
START TIME:	21 minutes, 00 seconds
START CUE:	Car drives across a bridge.

END TIME:	23 minutes, 30 seconds
END CUE:	Bruce returns to his wrecked car.
DURATION:	2 minutes, 30 seconds

Overview: Bruce prays for a sign from God, completely ignoring the actual physical signs warning him to stop. Bruce desperately prays for a miracle, and rams his car into a light post. He yells at God for not doing his job.

Illustration: Are you too self-absorbed to see the signs God sends your way? It's not that God doesn't talk to his people anymore, but that we miss the message. Help your young people spot God's signs so they don't wreck unnecessarily.

Questions:
- **Do you believe God has ever given you a sign? If so, what was it?**
- Read Mark 8:1-13. **Why didn't Jesus give the Pharisees a sign when they asked?**
- **How could the Pharisees possibly miss the feeding of over 4,000 people as a sign?**
- **What is God's purpose behind "signs"?**
- **How do people know when they're receiving a sign from God or when it's simply a lucky coincidence?**

Sin | I CAN'T CONTROL IT!

DRAMA	Title: **SPIDER-MAN 2**	PG-13
	Columbia Pictures, 2004	

Scripture: Romans 8:6-14

Alternate Takes: Flesh vs. Spirit (Romans 8:1-5), Temptation (Matthew 5:27-30)

DVD CHAPTER:	20
START TIME:	44 minutes, 45 seconds
START CUE:	The screen shows the exterior of the collapsed building.
END TIME:	47 minutes, 00 seconds
END CUE:	Doc Ock says, "Nothing will stand in our way! Nothing!"
DURATION:	2 minutes, 15 seconds

Overview: Doc Ock proclaims his mechanical arms should be destroyed—and then he hears the voices in his head. The inhibitor chip that kept the arms under his submission has been destroyed. Now the arms control Doc Ock, convincing him to engage in evil deeds.

Illustration: It's frightening how many people attach giant tentacles—sin—to their backs, expecting to maintain control with just a tiny little chip—their willpower. No one can play around with sin for long without getting bitten. Challenge your young people to identify the sinful "tentacles" grafted onto their lives and to throw the tentacles into the river.

Questions:

- What attitudes make a person believe they can maintain control over a dangerous situation or habit?
- Read Romans 8:6-14. **How would you paraphrase these verses?**
- Why might a person want to keep a sin around?
- How can you root a sin out of your life before it grows roots and protect yourself from allowing any new sin to grow?

Spiritual Disciplines | PRACTICE MAKES PERFECT

DRAMA	Title: **SEABISCUIT** Universal Pictures, 2003	PG-13

Scripture: 1 Corinthians 9:24-27
Alternate Take: Habits (Hebrews 5:11-14)

DVD CHAPTER:	20
START TIME:	1 hour, 29 minutes, 15 seconds
START CUE:	A sign that reads "Track Rules" is shown on the screen.
END TIME:	1 hour, 30 minutes, 15 seconds
END CUE:	Seabiscuit races away in the dark.
DURATION:	1 minute

Overview: Tom takes Seabiscuit onto the track at night to practice breaking at the sound of the bell. They practice the start over and over until Seabiscuit develops the habit of leaping off the starting line.

Illustration: Christians must train like Seabiscuit in regard to spiritual disciplines such as Bible reading, fasting, meditation, and prayer. Followers of Jesus must learn how to become dedicated disciples—it doesn't happen overnight. By doing the work now, your young people will become thoroughbreds, ready to race easily around the track God lays out for them.

Questions:

- What are some difficult things you've practiced that have become easy?
- What are some things you can do to develop your faith and relationship with God?
- Read 1 Corinthians 9:24-27. **Do you approach your faith with the same focus as Paul? Why or why not?**
- Why doesn't God simply make us instantly Christ-like when we follow Jesus?
- What are some spiritual disciplines you can incorporate into your life?

Standing Up | YOU'LL HAVE TO GO THROUGH ME

DRAMA	Title: **WALKING TALL** MGM, 2004	PG-13

Scripture: Joshua 1:6-9

Alternate Takes: Indifference (James 2:15-16),
Sodom and Gomorrah (Genesis 19:1-13)

DVD CHAPTER:	16
START TIME:	44 minutes, 15 seconds
START CUE:	Vaughn says, "I don't deny anything."
END TIME:	45 minutes, 30 seconds
END CUE:	Vaughn returns to his seat.
DURATION:	1 minute, 15 seconds

Overview: Vaughn admits to fighting the corruption coming out of the casino. He remembers how townspeople used to walk tall. He promises to run for sheriff and ensure that no one will endure what he's suffered. That's when he displays the horrible torture scars on his chest.

Illustration: Sometimes it takes only one person willing to stand up for what's right to defeat evil and injustice. Inspire your young people to do what is right no matter the odds or consequences, resting firm in the truth that God will honor their quest for righteousness.

Questions:
- Have you ever seen one person stand up for what's right? If so, what happened?
- What kinds of things prevent people from standing up against evil?
- Read Joshua 1:6-9. Why can Christians stand up with confidence?
- How can Christians be "blessed peacemakers" while standing up for what's right?
- Where does God want you to stand up?

Stealing | IT'S ONLY CABLE TV

Title: **THE CABLE GUY**	
HUMOR	Columbia Pictures, 1996

PG-13

Scripture: Exodus 20:15

Alternate Take: Integrity (Daniel 6:3-5)

DVD CHAPTER:	3
START TIME:	11 minutes, 30 seconds
START CUE:	Chip walks away.
END TIME:	12 minutes, 45 seconds
END CUE:	Chip says, "I'll juice you up."
DURATION:	1 minute, 15 seconds

Overview: Steven asks the cable guy, Chip, if he'd hook him up with all the movie channels for free. Chip says that's illegal—Steven could be fined or jailed. Steven backtracks until Chip laughs, saying he was just messing with him.

Illustration: There are a lot of things people thing it's OK to steal today—downloading music, sneaking into movies, using answers from a neighbor's test, and so on. Attack *all* forms of stealing.

Questions:

- What are some other things like cable that people think is no big deal to steal?
- What is the social impact of stealing? What is the spiritual impact?
- Read Exodus 20:15. **Does God disapprove of all stealing equally, whether you burn a song illegally or steal a car? Why or why not?**
- How do people excuse breaking such a basic commandment?
- What will it take to make your life free of all theft?

Stewardship | WHO'S GETTING YOUR BEST?

Title: THE RAINMAKER	
HUMOR Paramount Pictures, 1997	**PG-13**

Scripture: Luke 16:1-13

Alternate Takes: False Prophets (Matthew 7:15-16),
Riches (Proverbs 3:9-10)

DVD CHAPTER:	4
START TIME:	12 minutes, 30 seconds
START CUE:	Mrs. Birdy opens the door.
END TIME:	14 minutes, 45 seconds
END CUE:	Mrs. Birdy says, "Cut, cut, cut!"
DURATION:	2 minutes, 15 seconds

Overview: Rudy discusses Mrs. Birdy's will. She wants to leave everything to a TV evangelist. Rudy encourages her to leave some to her family, but she won't hear of it.

Illustration: Instead of looking at their bank accounts as *theirs*, help your young people see them as *God's*. Everything we have is on loan, and God entrusts us to use it wisely for his glory. Since we can't take it with us, discuss how to please our generous heavenly Father with it while we can.

Questions:

- Do you think Mrs. Birdy was being a good manager of her money? Why or why not?
- Read Luke 16:1-13. **How did the steward prove to have rotten stewardship skills?**
- What was Jesus trying to teach through this parable?
- What makes being a good steward so difficult?
- How can you become a better steward of what God has blessed you with?

Substance Abuse | EVERYBODY'S DOING IT

Title: DICKIE ROBERTS: FORMER CHILD STAR	
HUMOR Paramount Pictures, 2003	**PG-13**

Scripture: Isaiah 28:5-7

Alternate Take: Peer Pressure (Proverbs 2:20-22)

DVD CHAPTER:	10
START TIME:	44 minutes, 15 seconds
START CUE:	Dickie closes the refrigerator door.
END TIME:	46 minutes, 00 seconds
END CUE:	Dickie puts root beer on the table.
DURATION:	1 minute, 45 seconds

Overview: Dickie thinks Sam is a wimp for only drinking root beer. When he was a kid, he did all kinds of drugs. He thinks putting things off is stupid—you can do whatever you want whenever you want. Sally tells Dickie that's why he's so messed up now.

Illustration: Dickie looks like he turned out to be a real winner for all his underage drinking, huh? Your students are probably sick to death of all the horror stories of potential death and destruction that might come with substance abuse. Instead, address the guaranteed spiritual damage that comes with even "social" drinking or drugging.

Questions:
- **What reasons do people have for abusing addictive substances?**
- **Do these substances meet their needs? Why or why not?**
- Read Isaiah 28:5-7. **What spiritual damage does substance abuse cause? What social damage?**
- **What safeguards can you set up so you don't use any addictive substances?**

Substitution | I DID IT

	Title: **HOLES**	
DRAMA	Walt Disney Pictures, 2003	**PG**

Scripture: Mark 10:45
Alternate Take: Sacrifice (Luke 22:14-16)

DVD CHAPTER:	14
START TIME:	54 minutes, 45 seconds
START CUE:	Mr. Sir enters his truck.
END TIME:	56 minutes, 45 seconds
END CUE:	Stanley walks to the truck.
DURATION:	2 minutes

Overview: Magnet steals Mr. Sir's bag of sunflower seeds. The stolen seeds get thrown in Stanley's hole when Mr. Sir returns. Stanley takes the rap for the theft, claiming he stole them.

Illustration: Stanley shows his nobility by substituting himself for the true culprits—and mirrors what Christ did for each of us on the cross. Discuss Jesus' amazing sacrifice as well as ways we can sacrifice for others.

Questions:
- **Have you ever substituted yourself or had someone else substitute themselves for you? If so, what happened?**

- Why does even the smallest act of substitution speak volumes?
- Read Mark 10:45. **Why did Jesus agree to substitute himself as a "ransom"?**
- What makes his act of substitution the single greatest act in history?
- What are some ways you can substitute yourself for others in everyday life?

Talents | IT TAKES ALL KINDS

HUMOR	Title: **LEMONY SNICKET'S A SERIES OF UNFORTUNATE EVENTS**	PG
	Paramount Pictures, 2004	

Scripture: 1 Peter 4:10-11
Alternate Take: Uniqueness (1 Corinthians 12:4-10)

DVD CHAPTER:	1
START TIME:	2 minutes, 30 seconds
START CUE:	A photo of Violet is shown on the screen.
END TIME:	4 minutes, 00 seconds
END CUE:	Sunny laughs.
DURATION:	1 minute, 30 seconds

Overview: The Boudelaire children boast unique talents. Violet is an accomplished inventor, Klaus remembers everything he reads, and the baby, Sunny, bites anything within mouth's reach.

Illustration: God endowed each and every person with unique talents—abilities that should be used to build his kingdom. Every talent is useful, and God brings different people together in the church so they can work together to produce extraordinary results they could never achieve alone.

Questions:
- Do you think your talents are valuable? Explain.
- What happens when someone in God's family doesn't use his or her skills?
- Read 1 Peter 4:10-11. **Do you feel as if you're using your talents to glorify God and to serve others? Explain.**
- What is one way you could use your talents to glorify God this week?
- How could you use those gifts in church on a regular basis?

Taming the Tongue | DOWN, BOY!

HUMOR	Title: **MEAN GIRLS**	PG-13
	Paramount Pictures, 2004	

Scripture: James 3:3-12
Alternate Takes: Encouragement (Ephesians 4:29-32),
Gossip (Psalm 141:3-4)

DVD CHAPTER:	15
START TIME:	1 hour, 10 minutes, 45 seconds
START CUE:	Ms. Norbury says, "Everyboby close your eyes."
END TIME:	1 hour, 11 minutes, 15 seconds
END CUE:	Ms. Norbury says, "Girl-on-girl crime."
DURATION:	30 seconds

Overview: Ms. Norbury asks the girls to close their eyes and raise their hands if someone has ever talked bad about them. Every hand is raised, and she lets them see how they've all been hurt. She asks them to close their eyes again and raise their hands if they've talked bad about someone else. The girls open their eyes to see that they're all guilty of "girl-on-girl" crime.

Illustration: You could probably do this in your very own youth group with similar results. People love to rip each other with their words. This incredibly destructive pastime must stop in order for the kingdom of God to grow and remain strong. Challenge your young people to put aside all of their gossip, slander, and cutting remarks, choosing to allow only love and encouragement to roll off their lips.

Questions:
- **Would you have raised your hand in that assembly? Why or why not?**
- **What is the most hurtful thing someone has said about you? What effect have those words had on you?**
- Read James 3:3-12. **What makes it so difficult for us to hold our tongues?**
- **What are some subtle ways our society encourages us to hurt people with our words?**
- **How can you learn to change your hurtful words into expressions of love and encouragement?**

Teamwork | ALL TOGETHER NOW

Title: **FINDING NEMO**		G
DRAMA	Walt Disney Pictures, 2003	

Scripture: Ecclesiastes 4:9-12
Alternate Take: Risk (Romans 16:3-4)

DVD CHAPTER:	28
START TIME:	1 hour, 26 minutes, 30 seconds
START CUE:	A net chases the fish.
END TIME:	1 hour, 29 minutes, 00 seconds
END CUE:	The fish swim free.
DURATION:	2 minutes, 30 seconds

Overview: Dory gets caught in a net with a ton of other fish. Nemo can save them, but Marlin doesn't want him to risk his life. Nemo insists it's the only way, and Marlin agrees. They convince all the fish to swim down in the same direction—and they break free.

123

Illustration: Wouldn't it be great if the church would respond this quickly to crisis, immediately swimming the same direction to achieve great and mighty things for the kingdom of God? Remind your students that it *is* possible, and they must put aside their selfish ambitions to work as one with the body of Christ to see it happen.

Questions:

- **What are the advantages of working as a team? What are the disadvantages?**
- Read Ecclesiastes 4:9-12. **Why doesn't God give us all the tools we need to get the job done on our own?**
- **How does teamwork make the church grow stronger? How does it glorify God?**
- **How can we improve our teamwork as a ministry?**
- **How can you personally become a better teammate this week?**

Temptation | RUN!

	Title: **THE INCREDIBLES**	**PG**
HUMOR	Walt Disney Pictures, 2004	

Scripture: Genesis 39:1-20
Alternate Take: Talents (Matthew 25:14-29)

DVD CHAPTER:	23
START TIME:	1 hour, 24 minutes, 00 seconds
START CUE:	Dash and Violet are surrounded.
END TIME:	1 hour, 25 minutes, 45 seconds
END CUE:	Dash says, "I'm alive!"
DURATION:	1 minute, 45 seconds

Overview: Evil goons surround Dash. Violet reminds him of Mom's command to run, and he does just that, speeding through the forest at an unbelievable clip.

Illustration: This scene presents a simple concept when it comes to temptation—run! There's no better response to temptation when it slithers in to seduce us. Challenge your youth to emulate Dash when they come face to face with such compromising situations. Running away isn't chicken. It's the best defense against sin.

Questions:

- **Why is it sometimes prudent to run, even though there's nothing to fear with God?**
- **How do you know when to run and when God wants you to fight?**
- Read Genesis 39:1-20. **Why did God let Joseph get thrown in jail if he did the right thing?**
- **Is it a sin to be tempted? Why or why not?**
- **What are some ways you can strengthen and guard yourself against temptation besides running?**

Temptation of Christ | SATAN, GET BEHIND ME

DRAMA	Title: **SPIDER-MAN**	PG-13
	Columbia Pictures, 2002	

Scripture: Matthew 4:1-11
Alternate Take: Serving Others (1 Peter 4:10-11)

DVD CHAPTER:	21
START TIME:	1 hour, 15 minutes, 45 seconds
START CUE:	The Green Goblin says, "Wake up!"
END TIME:	1 hour, 17 minutes, 30 seconds
END CUE:	The Green Goblin flies away.
DURATION:	1 minute, 45 seconds

Overview: The Green Goblin attempts to convince Spider-Man to join him. He says the city doesn't care about him, so they should take it over together.

Illustration: Satan tried to convince our Savior to take a different, less painful route in life. Jesus stood firm, refusing to compromise God's plan to reconcile sinful humanity to the loving creator. Explore Jesus' temptation, and help your youth find both comfort and courage in their Lord's actions.

Questions:
- How is this movie scene similar to Jesus' temptation in the wilderness? How is it different?
- Read Matthew 4:1-11. What was the devil really tempting Jesus with at each stage of the story?
- How was Jesus able to withstand the temptations of the devil?
- What can we learn from this passage about Jesus? the devil? temptation?

Testing | WILL YOU PASS?

DRAMA	Title: **THE RECRUIT**	PG-13
	Touchstone Pictures, 2003	

Scripture: 2 Corinthians 13:5-6
Alternate Takes: Perseverance (1 Corinthians 9:24-27),
Trials (Matthew 7:24-27)

DVD CHAPTER:	7
START TIME:	42 minutes, 45 seconds
START CUE:	James gets dragged inside.
END TIME:	45 minutes, 15 seconds
END CUE:	James says, "Everything is a test."
DURATION:	2 minutes, 30 seconds

Overview: James gets kidnapped and placed in an isolated chamber where he's beaten, interrogated and starved. His captors question him about the CIA, but James won't respond, believing it's all a test.

Illustration: God doesn't hand out essay tests, but the sticky stuff of hard-knock life. It's amidst the trials that God molds and shapes us into the image of his perfect Son. Help your young people find the comfort and joy of God's promises in the midst of the harshest tests.

Questions:
- **Do you feel like faith comes easily to you, or is it a constant test? Explain.**
- Read 2 Corinthians 13:5-6. **Why would Paul recommend we test ourselves?**
- **How does a person put these verses into practice?**
- **What would be the desired results of testing one's faith?**
- **Will you try to test your faith in the future? Why or why not?**

Time | HOW DO YOU USE IT?

Title: **ABOUT A BOY**	
HUMOR Universal Pictures, 2002	**PG-13**

Scripture: Galatians 6:9-10
Alternate Take: Priorities (Psalm 1)

DVD CHAPTER:	8
START TIME:	29 minutes, 45 seconds
START CUE:	Will hooks up a cappuccino machine.
END TIME:	30 minutes, 30 seconds
END CUE:	The phone rings.
DURATION:	45 seconds

Overview: Will explains how he divides life into units of time that he fills with activities. He concludes he has a full life even though his activities are foolishly wasteful.

Illustration: We always talk about stewardship of our money, but how about our time? It's a precious gift given by God that we should protect and dispense wisely. Challenge your teens to examine how they use their time and discover ways to utilize larger and larger chunks for advancing God's kingdom.

Leader Tip: *This clip shows Will searching the Internet for pictures of women. This could be a great opportunity to challenge your youth about the time they spend on the Internet and whether or not that time is spent in a way that honors God.*

Questions:
- **Do you think Will's life is a good one to emulate? Why or why not?**
- **What kinds of activities do you consider to be a waste of time? Explain.**
- Read Galatians 6:9-10. **What makes time the most precious commodity on the planet?**
- **What should be the focus of our time?**
- **What changes must you make to your schedule so that you can make better use of your time?**

Trials | FUMBLE AROUND FOR A WHILE

DRAMA

Title: **RAY**

Universal Pictures, 2004

PG-13

Scripture: Psalm 28

Alternate Takes: God's Love (Psalm 37:28), Perseverance (Genesis 32:24-32)

DVD CHAPTER:	13
START TIME:	1 hour, 9 minutes, 30 seconds
START CUE:	Young Ray trips on a rocking chair.
END TIME:	1 hour, 12 minutes, 00 seconds
END CUE:	Mom says, " 'Cause I'm happy."
DURATION:	2 minutes, 30 seconds

Overview: Ray falls down and cries to his mom for help. She remains silent, so Ray starts listening. He makes his way around the room safely until he hears and catches a cricket. His mom hugs him close, happy with his success.

Illustration: Sometimes, for our own good, God remains silent when we cry out so that we learn to stand on our own and build muscles necessary for our spiritual growth. Encourage your young people to trust that God knows what he's doing, even when their trials leave them fumbling in the dark.

Questions:
- Was Ray's mom being cruel here? Why or why not?
- Has God ever remained silent when you cried out for help? If so, what happened?
- Read Psalm 28. Why does God sometimes remain silent when we cry out to him?
- How can we know that God is still there when he's silent?
- What hope can you cling for comfort to during a time of trial?

Trust | HOW CAN I?

DRAMA

Title: **LEGALLY BLONDE 2: RED, WHITE & BLONDE**

MGM, 2003

PG-13

Scripture: Psalm 13

Alternate Take: Questions (Job 30:20)

DVD CHAPTER:	24
START TIME:	57 minutes, 30 seconds
START CUE:	The Lincoln Memorial is shown on the screen.
END TIME:	58 minutes, 30 seconds
END CUE:	Elle says, "I did."
DURATION:	1 minute

Overview: Elle enters the Lincoln Memorial. She questions Abraham Lincoln's honesty and capacity to trust. She finds trusting the country, system, and herself incredibly difficult.

S-Z

Themes

Illustration: Trust can be an incredibly difficult thing to build in people—especially when others continually disappoint them. Turn your students toward God—to seek and to trust in him alone so they will have the foundation to place their faith in others as well.

Questions:
- **Do you find it difficult to trust others? God? Explain.**
- **What happened the last time someone abused or lost your trust?**
- Read Psalm 13. **How can we place complete trust in an invisible God who sometimes remains silent?**
- **Does it seem fair that we must place complete trust in an invisible God? Why or why not?**
- **How can you strengthen your trust in God?**

Truth | IT DOESN'T CHANGE

DRAMA	Title: **CHASING LIBERTY**	PG-13
	Warner Brothers, 2004	

Scripture: Zechariah 8:16-17
Alternate Take: Deceit (Proverbs 24:28)

DVD CHAPTER:	10
START TIME:	35 minutes, 00 seconds
START CUE:	Ben slides down the roof.
END TIME:	36 minutes, 00 seconds
END CUE:	Ben laughs.
DURATION:	1 minute

Overview: Ben and Anna watch a movie in which Paris deceives Helen. Anna launches into her theory that lying isn't always bad and the truth isn't always good. What's important is how you make people feel.

Illustration: She lies! The truth *is* important and shouldn't depend on the potential hurt feelings of others. Feelings heal when confronted by the truth, and the truth never changes. Confront the popular philosophy espoused by this scene, clearly explaining God's desire concerning truth.

Questions:
- **Do you agree with Anna's statement? Why or why not?**
- **Why is there so much debate over truth if it's supposed to be universal?**
- Read Zechariah 8:16-17. **How does one discern the truth?**
- **Are we supposed to be brutally honest with everyone about everything? Explain.**
- **Where do you need to become more truthful, and how will you do that?**

Unconditional Love | WHAT HAVE YOU DONE FOR ME LATELY?

HUMOR	Title: **Austin Powers in Goldmember**	PG-13
	New Line Cinema, 2002	

Scripture: Romans 8:35-39

Alternate Takes: Cliques (Isaiah 25:6-9), Favoritism (James 2:1-4),
Siblings (Genesis 25:21-26)

DVD CHAPTER:	9
START TIME:	52 minutes, 45 seconds
START CUE:	Scott enters.
END TIME:	54 minutes, 30 seconds
END CUE:	Mini Me rolls his chair backward.
DURATION:	1 minute, 45 seconds

Overview: Scott gives Dr. Evil some sharks with laser beams on their heads. Dr. Evil has Scott sit beside him, moving Mini Me down. Dr. Evil tells everyone to leave the room, and then lets everyone stay…but Mini Me.

Warning: Dr. Evil uses the word frickin' during this clip, which may be offensive to some.

Illustration: It's a good thing God doesn't operate like this. We're supposed to copy his example of unconditional love—remaining constant and loyal in our love, refusing to modify it based on what we receive in return. Challenge your students to examine their hearts and cut any of the strings they have attached to the love they have for others.

Questions:
- Have you ever experienced conditional love? If so, what happened?
- What makes conditional love so hurtful?
- Read Romans 8:35-39. **How can God possibly love us unconditionally, no matter what?**
- What effects should God's unconditional love have on our lives and faith?
- What steps can we take to show unconditional love to our families? our church?

Works | I DON'T NEED ANY HELP

HUMOR	Title: **MATCHSTICK MEN**
	Warner Brothers, 2003

PG-13

Scripture: Romans 3:19-28

Alternate Take: Holiness (Hebrews 10:10-14)

DVD CHAPTER:	4
START TIME:	12 minutes, 15 seconds
START CUE:	Roy pulls out a vacuum cleaner.
END TIME:	13 minutes, 15 seconds
END CUE:	Roy blows the last bit clean.
DURATION:	1 minute

Overview: Roy embarks on a feverish mission to completely clean his home. He scrubs everything from top to bottom, ultimately resorting to using a toothbrush to reach the tiniest areas—all while smoking cigarettes.

Illustration: We can toil endlessly, trying to clean up our mess, but we're "smoking" the whole way, leaving (often unintentional) waste in our wake. Challenge your young people to lay their personal "cleaning supplies" down and receive God's grace as the perfect purification for their soiled lives. Only faith in Christ's redemptive work on the cross will bring them close to God.

Questions:

- How does the world promote the belief that people can work toward perfection?
- How are they actually "smoking" while trying to "clean up" their lives under their own power?
- Read Romans 3:19-28. What kinds of works do people think will get them to heaven?
- Why would a person still try to enter heaven based on their works instead of simply having faith in Christ?
- Where is the proper balance between faith and works, and what must you do to achieve that balance?

Wounds | DON'T PUT THEM DOWN

Title: **SEABISCUIT**		PG-13
DRAMA	Universal Pictures, 2003	

Scripture: Ephesians 4:31-32
Alternate Take: The Church (Galatians 6:9-10)

DVD CHAPTER:	7
START TIME:	31 minutes, 00 seconds
START CUE:	A man leads out a horse.
END TIME:	32 minutes, 00 seconds
END CUE:	Tom pets the horse.
DURATION:	1 minute

Overview: Men try to hold down a horse with a fractured foot. The men plan to shoot him, but Tom convinces them to let him have the horse. Then Tom soothes him, saving the horse from death.

Illustration: If hurting people can't turn to Jesus, where can they go? The church should be a hospital for those with fractured souls. Challenge your students to be compassionate and caring to any of the hurting people they meet, offering a spiritual salve for people's pain.

Questions:

- Do you think wounded, hurting people receive good treatment when they come to church? Explain.
- What kinds of "wounds" do Christians sometimes turn away from, refusing to help? Why?
- Read Ephesians 4:31-32. How did Christ show compassion to the wounded people of the world?
- Why should the church be the best place in the world to bring these people?
- What are some practical ways we can become more caring for the hurting people who enter our church?

MOVIE
BACKGROUND
INDEX

13 Going on 30 (PG-13) Columbia Pictures, 2004 .... **19**
Jenna (Jennifer Garner) wishes on her thirteenth birthday that she was 30—and opens her eyes to find it so!

50 First Dates (PG-13) Columbia Pictures, 2004 .... **114**
Commitment-phobe Henry (Adam Sandler) falls in love with Lucy (Drew Barrymore), whose memory-damaging head injury forces him to win her heart every day.

About a Boy (PG-13) Universal Pictures, 2002 .... **110, 126**
Self-absorbed bachelor Will (Hugh Grant) has his perfectly selfish little world turned upside down when lonely 12-year-old Marcus (Nicholas Hoult) forces his way inside.

The Alamo (PG-13) Touchstone Pictures, 2004 .... **85**
Davy Crockett (Billy Bob Thornton), Jim Bowie (Jason Patric), Col. William Travis (Patrick Wilson), and less than 200 desperate men defend the Alamo against thousands of Mexican soldiers led by Gen. Santa Ana.

Along Came Polly (PG-13) Universal Pictures, 2004 .... **98**
Anal-retentive risk-assessment analyst Reuben (Ben Stiller) leaps outside his comfort zone by dating free-spirit Polly (Jennifer Aniston).

Anger Management (PG-13) Columbia Pictures, 2003 .... **27**
Mild-mannered pushover Dave Buznik (Adam Sandler) gets sentenced to anger management therapy with Dr. Buddy Rydell (Jack Nicholson), a wildly unorthodox therapist.

Antwone Fisher (PG-13) Fox Searchlight, 2002 .... **25, 56**
Dr. Davenport (Denzel Washington) peels away layers of the tortured childhood endured by angry Naval sailor Antwone Fisher (Derek Luke).

The Apostle (PG-13) Universal Pictures, 1997 .... **18, 71**
Pentecostal preacher Sonny (Robert Duvall) runs from the law in Texas and starts a thriving church in rural Louisiana.

Armageddon (PG-13) Touchstone Pictures, 1998 .... **36, 95, 106**
Harry Stamper (Bruce Willis) leads his rowdy team of drillers into space to destroy an asteroid that threatens to wipe out life on earth.

Austin Powers in Goldmember (PG-13) New Line Cinema, 2002 .... **128**
Austin Powers (Mike Myers) must rescue his dad Nigel (Michael Caine) from Dr. Evil while also preventing Goldmember from destroying the planet.

The Aviator (PG-13) Miramax Films, 2004 . . . . **81**
A biopic that tracks famed billionaire Howard Hughes' (Leonardo DiCaprio) extravagant, trail-blazing life—breaking the around-the-world flight record, making blockbuster films, and romancing Hollywood beauties—until his increasingly bizarre obsessive-compulsive behavior derails it.

Barbershop (PG-13) MGM, 2002 . . . . **67**
Calvin (Ice Cube) struggles over whether to sell his dad's barbershop—a neighborhood institution and home to its loyal customers and misfit employees.

Barbershop 2: Back in Business (PG-13) MGM, 2004 . . . . **29**
Nappy Cutz, a fancy chain, opens across the street, and Calvin (Ice Cube) fights to keep his landmark barbershop open.

Bend It Like Beckham (PG-13) Fox Searchlight, 2002 . . . . **71, 89**
Jess Bhamra (Parminder Nagra) lies to her strictly orthodox Sikh parents so she can follow her dreams of playing soccer.

Big Fish (PG-13) Columbia Pictures, 2003 . . . . **34, 79**
An embittered son, Will (Billy Crudup), desperately wants his cancer-stricken father, Edward Bloom (Albert Finney), to tell the truth about his past, leaving out all his elaborately colorful tall-tales, so Will can get to know who Edward really is.

Billy Madison (PG-13) Universal Pictures, 1995 . . . . **52**
Spoiled rich kid Billy Madison (Adam Sandler) must graduate high school (by repeating every grade) to gain his inheritance.

Blue Crush (PG-13) Universal Pictures, 2002 . . . . **59, 61**
Anne Marie (Kate Bosworth) dreams of winning the Pipe Masters competition, but fights distractions from her fear of failure and a budding relationship with football player Matt Tollman (Matthew Davis).

The Bourne Identity (PG-13) Universal Pictures, 2002 . . . . **67**
Amnesiac Jason Bourne (Matt Damon) sets out with only his incredible combat skills and wit to uncover his identity as well as figure out who keeps trying to kill him.

The Bourne Supremacy (PG-13) Universal Pictures, 2004 . . . . **60**
Amnesiac Jason Bourne (Matt Damon) gets dragged out of hiding by the CIA, forced to race across Europe, piecing together his memories as well as the treacherous plot for which he was framed.

Movie Background INDEX

Bringing Down the House (PG-13) Touchstone Pictures, 2003 . . . . **101**
Workaholic lawyer Peter Sanderson (Steve Martin) has life turned upside down when his Internet blind date, convicted felon Charlene Morton (Queen Latifah), insinuates herself into his orderly life.

Bruce Almighty (PG-13) Universal Pictures, 2003 . . . . **53, 86, 95, 116**
Self-centered newscaster Bruce Nolan (Jim Carrey) blames God for his horrible luck. God (Morgan Freeman) responds by giving Bruce all his power so he can do the job better.

The Cable Guy (PG-13) Columbia Pictures, 1996. . . . . **119**
Steven (Matthew Broderick) asks the Cable Guy (Jim Carrey) for some free channels, and gets a psychotic new "best friend" instead.

The Cat in the Hat (PG) Universal Pictures, 2003 . . . . **38**
The ultra-mischievous, magical Cat (Mike Meyers) leads rebellious Conrad (Spencer Breslin) and his perfectionist sister Sally (Dakota Fanning) in ignoring their mandate to keep the house clean.

Catch Me If You Can (PG-13) DreamWorks, 2002 . . . . **10, 42**
Charismatic teen con-artist Frank Abagnale Jr. (Leonardo DiCaprio) successfully impersonates a pilot, an emergency room doctor, and an attorney—all with tenacious FBI agent Carl Hanratty (Tom Hanks) in hot pursuit for Frank's millions of dollars in forged checks.

Chasing Liberty (PG-13) Warner Brothers, 2004. . . . . **128**
Anna Foster (Mandy Moore), 18-year-old daughter of the U.S. president, ditches her Secret Service entourage for a European adventure with handsome British photographer Ben Calder (Matthew Goode).

Cheaper by the Dozen (PG) 20th Century Fox, 2003. **49**
Tom Baker (Steve Martin) uproots his wife and 12 kids and transplants them to the big city, causing major chaos for all.

Chicago (PG-13) Miramax Films, 2002 . . . . **63, 79**
Roxie Hart (Renée Zellweger) uses her ample charms and slick defense lawyer, Billy Flynn (Richard Gere), to become a media darling in 1920s Chicago after shooting her lover.

Coach Carter (PG-13) Paramount Pictures, 2005 . . . . **37**
Ken Carter (Samuel L. Jackson) takes over as coach of the unruly, disrespectful Richmond High basketball team, demanding they live up to a code of conduct—including passing grades—if they want to play.

Daddy Day Care (PG) Columbia Pictures, 2003. . . . . **99**
Charlie Hinton (Eddie Murphy) loses his job and opens a day care for a dozen precocious children.

Daredevil (PG-13) 20th Century Fox, 2003 . . . . **74**
Blind lawyer Matt Murdock (Ben Affleck) defends the innocent by day, and hands out vigilante justice by night as the Daredevil.

Diary of a Mad Black Woman (PG-13) Lions Gate Films, 2005. . . . . **100**
Helen (Kimberly Elise) reconnects with her family after being booted out of her 18-year marriage by her two-timing husband, Charles (Steve Harris). She stays with her grandmother, Madea (Tyler Perry), finds the love of gentle Orlando (Shemar Moore), and seeks God's help to extend forgiveness.

Dickie Roberts: Former Child Star (PG-13) Paramount Pictures, 2003. . . . . **120**
Former child star Dickie Roberts (David Spade) pays a family to give him the childhood he never had.

Die Another Day (PG-13) MGM, 2002 . . . . **43**
British secret agent James Bond (Pierce Brosnan) goes rogue, tracking down a ruthless terrorist with the help of exotic and deadly agent Jinx (Halle Berry).

Dodgeball: A True Underdog Story (PG-13) 20th Century Fox, 2004. . . . . **76, 111**
Peter (Vince Vaughn) leads a team of losers into an extreme dodgeball tournament to save their gym from a hostile takeover by White Goodman (Ben Stiller), a fitness-club mogul.

Drumline (PG-13) 20th Century Fox, 2002 . . . . **12**
Freshman Devon Miles (Nick Cannon) works incredibly hard to please martinet band instructor Dr. Lee (Orlando Jones) and find his place on a Southern university's marching band's drumline.

Elf (PG) New Line Cinema, 2003. . . . . **46**
Buddy (Will Ferrell) learns that he's not truly an elf, and journeys to New York City in search of his biological father Walter (James Caan).

The Emperor's Club (PG-13) Universal Pictures, 2002 . . . . **23**
Classics professor William Hundert (Kevin Kline) attempts to mold his St. Benedict students into men of principle and character.

The Fighting Temptations (PG-13) Paramount Pictures, 2003. . . . . **94**
A slick, cash-strapped, New York ad man, Darrin Hill (Cuba Gooding

Movie Background INDEX

Jr.) must lead the Beulah church choir into a competition, the Gospel Explosion, in order to claim a $150,000 inheritance.

Finding Nemo (G) Walt Disney Pictures, 2003 . . . . **27, 123**
Worry-wart father Marlin (Albert Brooks) must swim across the ocean to Sydney when his only son, Nemo (Alexander Gould), gets snatched by a scuba-diving dentist.

Finding Neverland (PG) Miramax Films, 2004 . . . . **16**
Playwright J.M. Barrie (Johnny Depp) experiences an explosion of imagination as a result of his relationship with widow Sylvia Davies (Kate Winslet) and her four sons, who serve as inspiration for the play *Peter Pan*.

First Knight (PG-13) Columbia Pictures, 1995 . . . . **112**
Lancelot (Richard Gere) joins the Round Table of King Arthur (Sean Connery), and then steals his wife, Guinevere (Julia Ormond).

Frequency (PG-13) New Line Cinema, 2000 . . . . **58**
Somehow, John (Jim Caviezel) is able to communicate across 30 years with his dead father Frank (Dennis Quaid). He saves his father's life, but then they must reverse the consequences.

Friday Night Lights (PG-13) Universal Pictures, 2004 . . . . **91, 97**
Coach Gary Gaines (Billy Bob Thornton) and his team, the Permian High School football team, face the pressure and expectations of their city, families, and classmates while struggling for the championship.

Guess Who (PG-13) Columbia Pictures, 2005 . . . . **47**
Simon (Ashton Kutcher) meets his black fiancée's father, Percy (Bernie Mac), who's none too keen about his daughter Theresa (Zoe Saldana) falling in love with a wimpy white guy.

Hellboy (PG-13) Columbia Pictures, 2004 . . . . **65**
Hellboy (Ron Perlman), a demon child summoned from the dark side by the Nazis, leads a team of "freaks," including flame-throwing femme fatale Liz (Selma Blair) and amphibious telepath Abe (Doug Jones) on top-secret FBI missions that involve monsters, the occult, and the unexplained.

Hero (PG-13) Miramax Films, 2004 . . . . **103**
A nameless warrior (Jet Li) appears before the King of Qin with a gift—proof that he's killed three deadly assassins who sought to end the king's life. Nameless then relates the story of his heroic journey to defeat them.

Hitch (PG-13) Columbia Pictures, 2005 . . . . **15**
Date doctor Hitch (Will Smith) helps poor shlubs make impossible love connections, but fumbles in his own relationship with Sara (Eva Mendes).

Holes (PG) Walt Disney Pictures, 2003. . . . . **28, 103, 121**
Stanley Yelnats (Shia Labeouf) gets unjustly sentenced to juvenile detention at Camp Green Lake and digging endless holes. Stanley resolves to uncover the mystery when he realizes that the warden (Sigourney Weaver) really seeks a lost treasure.

Hollywood Homicide (PG-13) Columbia Pictures, 2003 . . . . **70**
Grizzled veteran detective Joe Gavilan (Harrison Ford) and his young, yoga-loving partner K.C. Calden (Josh Hartnett) must find the murderer of an up-and-coming rap group.

Hook (PG) TriStar Pictures, 1991 . . . . **30**
Grown up Peter (Robin Williams) must remember his former life in Neverland when Captain Hook (Dustin Hoffman) kidnaps his children.

Hotel Rwanda (PG-13) MGM, 2004. . . . . **69**
Hotel manager Paul Rusesabagina (Don Cheadle) shelters refugees in a luxury hotel when the Hutus begin slaughtering the Tutsis in Rwanda, bartering and bribing any way he can to preserve more than 1,200 lives.

The Hours (PG-13) Paramount Pictures, 2002. . . . . **63**
The lives of three women from three different eras intersect. Novelist Virginia Woolf (Nicole Kidman), '50s housewife Laura Brown (Julianne Moore), and modern-day book editor Clarissa Vaughan (Meryl Streep) all seek happiness in life.

How to Lose a Guy in 10 Days (PG-13) Paramount Pictures, 2003 . . . . **77**
Love collides when Benjamin (Matthew McConaughey) bets he can make a woman fall in love in 10 days while magazine columnist Andie (Kate Hudson) decides to prove she can repel a boyfriend in 10 days.

Hulk (PG-13) Universal Pictures, 2003 . . . . **14, 109**
Dr. Bruce Banner (Eric Bana) transforms into Hulk—a mean, green rage-machine—whenever he gets angry.

I Am David (PG) Lions Gate Films, 2003 . . . . **73**
Twelve-year-old David (Ben Tibber) escapes a Communist concentration camp with only a compass, a piece of bread, and a sealed letter. He can trust no one on his lonely trek across the European countryside to safety in Denmark.

Movie Background INDEX

The Incredibles (PG) Walt Disney Pictures, 2004 . . . . **124**
Bob (Craig T. Nelson) and Helen (Holly Hunter) must become superheroes
Mr. Incredible and Elastigirl once again when Syndrome (Jason Lee), a new
super-villain, threatens their family and the world.

Intolerable Cruelty (PG-13) Universal Pictures, 2003 . . . . **38**
Gold digger Marilyn Rexroth (Catherine Zeta-Jones) seeks revenge on Miles
Massey (George Clooney), the slick lawyer who beat her in court and wants
to steal her heart.

Jonah: A VeggieTales Movie (G) Artisan, 2002 . . . . **97, 101**
The Pirates Who Don't Do Anything relate the amazing tale of the prophet
Jonah, whose wayward path (via a whale) eventually takes the word of the
Lord to the cluelessly wicked people of Nineveh.

Joshua (G) Artisan, 2002 . . . . **83**
Joshua (Tony Goldwyn), a mysterious carpenter, arrives in a small town and
begins to change the hearts and minds of everyone he meets with his love,
wisdom, and apparent miracles.

Just Married (PG-13) 20th Century Fox, 2003. . . . . **29**
Tom (Ashton Kutcher) and Sarah (Brittany Murphy) fall madly in love and
plunge into marriage against the advice of family and friends. Their wedded
bliss hits speed bumps during a nightmarish European honeymoon.

K-19: The Widowmaker (PG-13) Paramount Pictures, 2002 . . . . **48, 81**
Based on a real-life incident involving an untested Russian submarine whose
maiden voyage in 1961 forced the crew to lay their lives on the line to prevent a catastrophic nuclear tragedy.

Ladder 49 (PG-13) Touchstone Pictures, 2004. . . . . **105**
Jack Morrison (Joaquin Phoenix) thinks back on his life as a fireman while
trapped in a burning building awaiting rescue.

Lara Croft Tomb Raider: The Cradle of Life (PG-13) Paramount Pictures, 2003 . . . . **78**
Lara Croft (Angelina Jolie) races to recover Pandora's Box before evil bio-
chemist Jonathan Reiss (Ciarán Hinds) can unleash its devastating disease
upon the world.

Legally Blonde 2: Red, White & Blonde (PG-13) MGM, 2003. . . . . **21, 99, 127**
Elle Woods (Reese Witherspoon) prances onto Capitol Hill to fight against
the evils of animal testing.

Lemony Snicket's A Series of Unfortunate Events
(PG) Paramount Pictures, 2004 . . . . **122**
The orphaned Boudelaire children land in the care of Count Olaf (Jim Carrey), the treacherous man trying to steal their inheritance.

Les Misérables (PG-13) Columbia Pictures, 1998 . . . . **72, 75, 82**
Noble-hearted ex-con Jean Valjean (Liam Neeson) hides from the relentless Inspector Javert (Geoffrey Rush) in order to keep his promise to raise young Cosette (Claire Danes).

The Lord of the Rings:
The Return of the King (PG-13) New Line Cinema, 2003 . . . . **33, 39, 50**
Gandalf (Ian McKellen) and company fight off the orc hordes while Frodo (Elijah Wood) attempts to destroy the One Ring in the fires of Mordor.

The Lord of the Rings: The Two Towers (PG-13) New Line Cinema, 2002 . . . . **92**
Frodo (Elijah Wood) and Sam (Sean Astin) continue their journey to Mordor to destroy the One Ring, while Aragorn (Viggo Mortensen) and company hold off Dark Lord Sauron's forces at Helm's Deep.

Maid in Manhattan (PG-13) Columbia Pictures, 2002 . . . . **62**
Single mother Marisa Ventura (Jennifer Lopez) works as a maid in a fancy New York hotel. When senatorial hopeful Christopher Marshall (Ralph Fiennes) mistakes Marissa for a guest, she hides her identity in hopes that their love can grow.

Malibu's Most Wanted (PG-13) Warner Brothers, 2003 . . . . **90**
Wealthy white boy Brad "B-Rad" Gluckman (Jamie Kennedy) acts like he's straight out of Compton. His father tries to teach him a lesson by hiring some actors to kidnap B-Rad and show him what real ghetto life is all about.

Master and Commander: The Far Side of the World
(PG-13) 20th Century Fox, 2003 . . . . **41, 53**
Captain Jack Aubrey (Russell Crowe) tests the limits of his men's loyalty and endurance in their quest to capture or sink a far superior French ship.

Matchstick Men (PG-13) Warner Brothers, 2003 . . . . **129**
Phobic con man Roy Waller (Nicholas Cage) has his perfectly ordered life thrown in confusion when Angela (Alison Lohman), a daughter he never knew existed, appears in the middle of his biggest con.

Mean Girls (PG-13) Paramount Pictures, 2004 . . . . **25, 122**
Cady Heron (Lindsay Lohan) joins the popular clique at school, The Plastics, and turns into the very thing she always hated—an extremely mean girl.

Movie Background INDEX

Meet the Fockers (PG-13) Universal Pictures, 2004 . . . . **110**
Greg (Ben Stiller) introduces stiff Jack (Robert DeNiro) and Dina Byrnes (Blythe Danner) to his crazy parents, Bernie (Dustin Hoffman) and Roz Focker (Barbara Streisand).

Men in Black II (PG-13) Columbia Pictures, 2002 . . . . **116**
Agent Jay (Will Smith) re-enlists Agent Kay (Tommy Lee Jones) to help him prevent evil alien Serleena (Lara Flynn Boyle) from destroying earth.

Million Dollar Baby (PG-13) Warner Brothers, 2004 . . . . **24, 44**
Frankie Dunn (Clint Eastwood) takes on a headstrong female boxer, Maggie Fitzgerald (Hilary Swank), guiding her toward a shot at the world championship.

Minority Report (PG-13) 20th Century Fox, 2002 . . . . **13, 96**
Detective John Anderton (Tom Cruise) heads the Department of Pre-Crime, a division that stops crime before it happens with the use of precognitive mutants. When the "pre-cogs" foresee Anderton murdering a stranger, he flees to clear his name.

Miracle (PG) Walt Disney Pictures, 2004 . . . . **58**
In 1980, U.S. hockey coach Herb Brooks (Kurt Russell) gathers a ragtag group of prideful, warring college players and molds them into a unified Olympic team that will face the unbeatable Russian squad.

Monsters, Inc. (G) Walt Disney Pictures, 2001 . . . . **51, 91**
Sulley (John Goodman) harvests screams from little children for energy. When a little girl follows him back into the monster world, Sulley and his best friend Mike (Billy Crystal) must return her before anyone finds out.

Mr. Deeds (PG-13) Columbia Pictures, 2002 . . . . **40, 69**
Small-town sweet dude Longfellow Deeds (Adam Sandler) lands in cutthroat New York with a $40 billion inheritance from an unknown uncle.

Mrs. Doubtfire (PG-13) 20th Century Fox, 1993 . . . . **85**
Daniel (Robin Williams) stays close to his children in the midst of his divorce by securing a job as their English nanny, Mrs. Doubtfire.

Napoleon Dynamite (PG) Fox Searchlight, 2004 . . . . **21, 34**
Napoleon Dynamite (Jon Heder) endures his tiresome brother, uncle, and high school, while working to get his friend, Pedro (Efren Ramirez), elected president of the student body.

National Treasure (PG) Walt Disney Pictures, 2004 . . . . **48**
Benjamin Gates (Nicolas Cage) uses a map on the back of the Declaration of Independence to recover an historical treasure.

Nicholas Nickleby (PG) MGM, 2002 . . . . **104**
Nicholas Nickleby (Charlie Hunnam), a virtuous young man, fights the social indignities and physical abuses suffered by his family and friends in turn-of-the-century England.

Ocean's 12 (PG-13) Warner Brothers, 2004 . . . . **108**
Danny Ocean (George Clooney) and the rest of the crew come out of retirement to pull a huge European heist after Terry Benedict (Andy Garcia) tracks them down and demands his money back—plus interest.

The Passion of the Christ (R) New Market Films, 2004 . . . . **11, 108**
Follow Jesus Christ (Jim Caviezel) on his redemptive path from the garden of Gethsemane to his brutal triumph on the cross at Calvary.

Peter Pan (PG) Universal Pictures, 2003 . . . . **42**
Peter Pan (Jeremy Sumpter), the boy who refuses to grow up, takes Wendy (Rachel Hurd-Wood) and her brothers to Neverland to join the Lost Boys and fight Captain Hook (Jason Isaacs) and his pirates.

Pirates of the Caribbean: The Curse of the Black Pearl
(PG-13) Walt Disney Pictures, 2003 . . . . **89**
Humble blacksmith Will Turner (Orlando Bloom) leaps into action when pirates kidnap his true love Elizabeth (Keira Knightley). He springs the notorious Captain Jack Sparrow (Johnny Depp) from jail to help rescue her from Capt. Barbossa (Geoffrey Rush) and his undead crew.

The Princess Diaries 2: Royal Engagement (G) Walt Disney Pictures, 2004 . . . . **113**
Princess Mia (Anne Hathaway) returns to Genovia ready to assume the throne from her grandmother—until she learns Genovian law mandates she must marry in order to become queen.

Rabbit-Proof Fence (PG) Miramax Films, 2002 . . . . **83, 107**
In 1931, Molly Craig (Everlyn Sampi) escapes with her two sisters from their re-education camp and leads them on foot 1,500 miles back to their home in the Australian Outback.

Radio (PG) Columbia Pictures, 2003 . . . . **64**
High school football coach, Jones (Ed Harris), takes an interest in Radio (Cuba Gooding Jr.), a mentally challenged young man who watches the team's practice every day.

Movie Background INDEX

The Rainmaker (PG-13) Paramount Pictures, 1997 . . . . **12, 44, 120**
Fresh-out-of-law-school idealist Rudy Baylor (Matt Damon) takes on a huge law firm and the corrupt insurance company they represent.

Raise Your Voice (PG) New Line Cinema, 2004 . . . . **87**
Terri Fletcher (Hilary Duff) leaves her small town for the stage of a prestigious performing arts school in Los Angeles.

Raising Helen (PG-13) Touchstone Pictures, 2004 . . . . **16**
Helen Harris (Kate Hudson) leaves her glamorous life as a fashion agent behind to raise her orphaned nephew and two nieces.

Ray (PG-13) Universal Pictures, 2004. . . . . **127**
The true story of superstar Ray Charles (Jamie Foxx), his incredible musical career, messed-up personal life, and crippling drug addiction.

The Recruit (PG-13) Touchstone Pictures, 2003. . . . . **125**
James Clayton (Colin Farrell) accepts an invitation from Walter Burke (Al Pacino) to become a spy for the CIA. As he gets deeper into the espionage, he can't tell whom to trust.

Robin Hood: Prince of Thieves (PG-13) Warner Brothers, 1991 . . . . **17**
Robin of Locksley (Kevin Costner) takes up vigilante style justice when he returns to England and finds the people oppressed under the vicious Sheriff of Nottingham (Alan Rickman).

The Rundown (PG-13) Universal Pictures, 2003 . . . . **23**
Recovery specialist Beck (The Rock) travels to the Amazon to capture and return Travis (Seann William Scott) to L.A. Only a golden idol, a ruthless slaver, and a beautiful revolutionary stand in the way.

The Santa Clause 2 (G) Walt Disney Pictures, 2002 . . . . **26, 106**
Santa (Tim Allen) must get married within one month or he will lose his job as Father Christmas.

Scary Movie 3 (PG-13) Dimension Films, 2003 . . . . **78**
TV news reporter Cindy Campbell (Anna Faris) discovers a horrible connection between crop circles and a deadly video in this silly spoof of modern horror movies.

School of Rock (PG-13) Paramount Pictures, 2003 . . . . **20, 62**
Dewey Finn (Jack Black) poses as a substitute teacher in an exclusive private school and transforms his fourth-grade class into a rock band.

The Scorpion King (PG-13) Universal Pictures, 2002 . . . . **32**
Mathayus (The Rock) attempts to overthrow evil King Memnon (Steven Brand), who's waging a bloodthirsty war across the ancient world.

Seabiscuit (PG-13) Universal Pictures, 2003 . . . . **55, 118, 130**
The true story of half-blind jockey Red Pollard (Tobey Maguire), unemployed trainer Tom Smith (Chris Cooper), and grieving millionaire Charles Howard (Jeff Bridges), which brings hope to the Depression era through their spunky racehorse Seabiscuit.

Shark Tale (PG) DreamWorks, 2004 . . . . **32**
Oscar (Will Smith) dreams of making it big. He teams up with Lenny (Jack Black), a timid shark, to pretend that he's a fearsome shark slayer and win the respect he craves.

Shattered Glass (PG-13) Lions Gate Films, 2003 . . . . **18**
The true story of Stephen Glass (Hayden Christensen) and his attempt to cover up his egregious fabrications while reporting for The New Republic magazine.

Shrek 2 (PG) DreamWorks, 2004 . . . . **46**
Shrek (Mike Myers) and Princess Fiona (Cameron Diaz) return from their honeymoon and visit her parents, the King and Queen of a Kingdom Far, Far Away, who aren't exactly happy with their new son-in-law.

Spider-Man (PG-13) Columbia Pictures, 2002 . . . . **51, 54, 125**
Peter Parker (Tobey Maguire) gets bitten by a radioactive spider, giving him super powers. He tries to learn his new skills, stop the evil plans of the Green Goblin (Willem Dafoe), and win the heart of his love Mary Jane Watson (Kirsten Dunst).

Spider-Man 2 (PG-13) Columbia Pictures, 2004 . . . . **65, 117**
Peter Parker (Tobey Maguire) hangs up his tights, but Doc Ock (Alfred Molina), a mechanically-tentacled menace, drags the web-slinger out of retirement.

The SpongeBob SquarePants Movie (PG) Paramount Pictures, 2004 . . . . **40**
SpongeBob (Tom Kenny) and Patrick (Bill Fagerbakke) must retrieve King Neptune's crown from deadly Shell City, or Mr. Krabs (Clancy Brown) will be executed.

Spy Kids 2: The Island of Lost Dreams (PG) Dimension Films, 2002 . . . . **14**
The Cortez siblings blast off for the Island of Lost Dreams, which is overrun by hybrid animal/monsters created by mad-scientist Romero (Steve Buscemi) to recover the Transmooker Device.

Spy Kids 3D: Game Over (PG) Dimension Films, 2003 . . . . **56**
Juni Cortez (Daryl Sabara) rejoins the top secret OSS agency to save his sister Carmen (Alexa Vega), who's trapped inside a virtual-reality video game.

Star Wars Episode II: Attack of the Clones (PG) 20th Century Fox, 2002 . . . . . **31, 68**
The plot thickens as Obi-Wan (Ewan McGregor) discovers a clone army while his young padawan Anakin Skywalker (Hayden Christensen) secretly marries Amidala (Natalie Portman) and takes a step closer to the Dark Side.

Stuck on You (PG-13) 20th Century Fox, 2003 . . . . **36**
Conjoined twins Bob (Matt Damon) and Walt (Greg Kinnear) pursue their dreams when they move to Hollywood—Walt for acting and Bob for the pen pal he loves.

The Sum of All Fears (PG-13) Paramount Pictures, 2002 . . . . **60**
CIA analyst Jack Ryan (Ben Affleck) stumbles onto a neo-Nazi plot to detonate a small nuclear bomb in the U.S. and provoke an all-out war with Russia.

Super Size Me (PG) Samuel Goldwyn Films, 2004 . . . . **35, 57**
A documentary depicting what happens to Morgan Spurlock's body when he eats McDonald's at every meal for 30 days straight.

Sweet Home Alabama (PG-13) Touchstone Pictures, 2002 . . . . **73**
New York fashion designer Melanie (Reese Witherspoon) must put her upcoming wedding to Andrew (Patrick Dempsey) on hold until she finalizes her divorce from childhood sweetheart Jake (Josh Lucas) in Pigeon Creek, Alabama.

The Terminal (PG-13) DreamWorks, 2004 . . . . **66, 76**
Viktor (Tom Hanks) must work and live in an airport terminal, unable to leave when his home country in Eastern Europe suffers a coup.

Two Brothers (PG) Universal Pictures, 2004. . . . . **93**
Separated twin tiger cubs spend years in very different forms of captivity, only to reunite in a daring escape attempt.

Uptown Girls (PG-13) MGM, 2003 . . . . **80**
Party girl Molly (Brittany Murphy) loses her entire fortune and must actually work for a living as a nanny for Lorraine "Ray" Schleine (Dakota Fanning), an uptight, 8-year-old germaphobe.

Walking Tall (PG-13) MGM, 2004 . . . . **118**
Special forces soldier Chris Vaughn (The Rock) vows to fight against the
powerful casino-owning, smut-peddling, and drug-selling Jay Hamilton Jr.
(Neal McDonough) by running for sheriff and standing firm with a mighty
piece of lumber by his side.

Waterworld (PG-13) Universal Pictures, 1995 . . . . **87**
The world has been covered with water, and Mariner (Kevin Costner) tries
to help Helen (Jeanne Tripplehorn) and her daughter find a mythical island
that is tattooed on the child's back.

Whale Rider (PG-13) Newmarket Films, 2002 . . . . **45**
Pai (Keisha Castle-Hughes), a young Maori girl, longs for the love and respect
of her grandfather Koro (Rawiri Paratene). He bristles when Pai challenges the
tribe's cultural traditions by seeking to join in the male rites of passage.

What a Girl Wants (PG) Warner Brothers, 2003 . . . . **10, 22**
Free-spirited American teen Daphne (Amanda Bynes) travels to England
to connect with the father she's never met—Lord Henry Dashwood (Colin
Firth). Her arrival sets up the ultimate fish out of water scenario.

What's Eating Gilbert Grape (PG-13) Paramount Pictures, 1993 . . . . **88**
Gilbert (Johnny Depp) must look after his mentally-challenged brother
Arnie (Leonardo DiCaprio) and their severely obese mother in a small town
where everyone knows everything about each other.

Win a Date With Tad Hamilton! (PG-13) DreamWorks, 2004 . . . . **102, 115**
Grocery clerk Rosalee (Kate Bosworth) wins the date of her dreams with
hunky movie star Tad Hamilton (Josh Duhamel), who, much to best friend
Pete's (Topher Grace) horror, follows her back to West Virginia.

X2: X-Men United (PG-13) 20th Century Fox, 2003 . . . . **84, 93, 113**
General William Stryker (Brian Cox) leads an aggressive witch-hunt against
mutants, looking to exterminate the X-Men, including Wolverine (Hugh
Jackman), Storm (Halle Berry), and Jean Grey (Famke Janssen).

SCRIPTURE INDEX

Genesis 1:27 . . . . **113**	Deuteronomy 15:7-11 . . . . **64**
Genesis 2:18-24 . . . . **49**	Deuteronomy 22:13-21 . . . . **113**
Genesis 2:20-25 . . . . **73**	Deuteronomy 30:19-20 . . . . **56**
Genesis 3:8-13 . . . . **103**	Deuteronomy 32:39 . . . . **44**
Genesis 19:1-13 . . . . **118**	Joshua 1:6-9 . . . . **118**
Genesis 20:1-13 . . . . **47**	Joshua 22:5 . . . . **35**
Genesis 25:21-26 . . . . **128**	Joshua 24:14-15 . . . . **23, 96**
Genesis 25:27-28 . . . . **50**	Ruth 1:8-18 . . . . **22**
Genesis 29:15-20 . . . . **79**	1 Samuel 1:9-17 . . . . **111**
Genesis 32:24-32 . . . . **127**	1 Samuel 6:13-19 . . . . **33**
Genesis 37:3-4 . . . . **50**	1 Samuel 14:1-14 . . . . **32, 105**
Genesis 39:1-20 . . . . **124**	1 Samuel 16:7 . . . . **19**
Genesis 39:5-12 . . . . **113**	1 Samuel 17:40-49 . . . . **89**
Exodus 2:11-14 . . . . **46**	1 Samuel 24:1-12 . . . . **103**
Exodus 3:7-9 . . . . **12**	2 Samuel 13:10-20 . . . . **74**
Exodus 4:11 . . . . **81**	2 Samuel 15:1-6 . . . . **102**
Exodus 16:1-3 . . . . **29**	1 Kings 17:17-24 . . . . **42**
Exodus 20:12 . . . . **89**	1 Chronicles 28:9 . . . . **60**
Exodus 20:15 . . . . **119**	2 Chronicles 25:19-22 . . . . **99**
Exodus 31:1-5 . . . . **34**	Ezra 9:5-9 . . . . **108**
Exodus 34:6-7 . . . . **56**	Nehemiah 9:5-6 . . . . **26**
Exodus 35:30–36:1 . . . . **14**	Nehemiah 9:24-31 . . . . **33**
Leviticus 5:17 . . . . **11**	Esther 3:5-6 . . . . **27**
Leviticus 6:1-5 . . . . **18**	Job 14:1-5 . . . . **31**
Leviticus 10:1-3 . . . . **38**	Job 27:2-4 . . . . **47**
Leviticus 19:11 . . . . **39, 67**	Job 30:20 . . . . **127**
Leviticus 19:31 . . . . **33**	Job 34:21-22 . . . . **60**
Numbers 20:2-5 . . . . **103**	Psalm 1 . . . . **126**
Deuteronomy 7:7-8 . . . . **58**	Psalm 6 . . . . **89**
Deuteronomy 10:17 . . . . **62**	Psalm 8 . . . . **45**
Deuteronomy 11:26-28 . . . . **53**	Psalm 8:6-8 . . . . **93**
Deuteronomy 13:6-8 . . . . **27**	Psalm 13 . . . . **127**

SCRIPTURE INDEX

Psalm 15. . . . . **29**

Psalm 25:1-5 . . . . **36**

Psalm 27:1-6 . . . . **66**

Psalm 28. . . . . **127**

Psalm 37:4-6 . . . . **40**

Psalm 37:5-7 . . . . **19**

Psalm 37:7 . . . . **68**

Psalm 37:28. . . . . **127**

Psalm 51:1-4 . . . . **51, 81, 84**

Psalm 68:5-6 . . . . **79**

Psalm 68:32-35. . . . . **32**

Psalm 72:1-7 . . . . **76**

Psalm 75:6-7 . . . . **97**

Psalm 77:11-20. . . . . **39**

Psalm 81:8-14 . . . . **87**

Psalm 94:19. . . . . **47**

Psalm 96:1-4 . . . . **69**

Psalm 98. . . . . **85**

Psalm 101:5-8 . . . . **38**

Psalm 103:13. . . . . **58**

Psalm 111:10. . . . . **51**

Psalm 118:6-9 . . . . **39**

Psalm 139:13-16. . . . . . . **10, 19, 79, 110**

Psalm 141:3-4 . . . . **122**

Psalm 146:5-10. . . . . **74**

Psalm 147:7-9 . . . . **29**

Psalm 149:1-5 . . . . **34**

Psalm 150:4-6 . . . . **15**

Proverbs 1:28-33. . . . . **96**

Proverbs 2:20-22. . . . . **120**

Proverbs 3:3-4 . . . . **75**

Proverbs 3:9-10. . . . . **120**

Proverbs 3:21-26. . . . . **51**

Proverbs 4:25-27. . . . . **70**

Proverbs 5:11-13. . . . . **114**

Proverbs 6:32-35. . . . . **100**

Proverbs 8:13. . . . . **41**

Proverbs 10:18-21. . . . . **30, 122**

Proverbs 11:2. . . . . **98**

Proverbs 11:14. **44**

Proverbs 11:24-25. . . . . **56**

Proverbs 12:18. **67**

Proverbs 13:4. . . . . **62**

Proverbs 13:5-7 . . . . **15**

Proverbs 13:24. **10**

Proverbs 14:21. . . . . **104**

Proverbs 14:31. . . . . **105**

Proverbs 15:18. **14**

Proverbs 15:21-22. . . . . **59, 68**

Proverbs 15:29. . . . . **116**

Proverbs 18:20-21. . . . . **61**

Proverbs 19:9. . . . . **29, 71**

Proverbs 20:1. . . . . **40**

Proverbs 22:1. . . . . **40, 102**

Proverbs 22:2. . . . . **62, 112**

Proverbs 23:4-5 . . . . **80**

Proverbs 23:19-21. . . . . **40, 57**

Proverbs 24:28. . . . . **128**

Proverbs 25:21-22. . . . . **75**

Proverbs 25:28. **14**

Proverbs 26:20-24. . . . . **61**

Proverbs 27:6-9 . . . . **12**

Proverbs 27:17. **41**

Proverbs 29:15. **38**

Proverbs 29:23. . . . .**46**

Ecclesiastes 4:1-6 . . . .**90**

Ecclesiastes 4:9-12 . . . .**123**

Ecclesiastes 7:9 . . . .**56**

Song of Songs 2:3-7 . . . .**73**

Song of Songs 3:1-5 . . . .**113, 115**

Isaiah 1:17 . . . .**63**

Isaiah 1:18 . . . .**62**

Isaiah 10:1-3 . . . .**69**

Isaiah 15:1-4 . . . .**55**

Isaiah 22:3-4 . . . .**107**

Isaiah 25:6-9 . . . .**128**

Isaiah 28:5-7 . . . .**120**

Isaiah 33:1-2 . . . .**17**

Isaiah 35:3-4 . . . .**42**

Isaiah 35:4-10 . . . .**13**

Isaiah 40:28-31 . . . .**67**

Isaiah 41:8-10 . . . .**16**

Isaiah 43:18-19 . . . .**35**

Isaiah 49:15-16 . . . .**53**

Isaiah 55:8-9 . . . .**48**

Isaiah 58:6-10 . . . .**72**

Isaiah 59:14-20 . . . .**104**

Jeremiah 1:5 . . . .**78**

Jeremiah 15:10-11 . . . .**28**

Jeremiah 23:23-24 . . . .**70**

Ezekiel 1:15-20 . . . .**78**

Ezekiel 3:4-7 . . . .**78**

Ezekiel 16:1-15 . . . .**60**

Daniel 6:3-5. . . . .**119**

Jonah 1:1-3 . . . .**97**

Micah 6:8 . . . .**74**

Zechariah 7:8-10 . . . .**84**

Zechariah 8:16-17. . . . .**38, 128**

Malachi 2:8-10 . . . .**90**

Matthew 3:11-12 . . . .**65**

Matthew 4:1-11 . . . .**125**

Matthew 5:1-12 . . . .**63**

Matthew 5:7 . . . .**37**

Matthew 5:9 . . . .**85**

Matthew 5:13-16 . . . .**23, 41, 69**

Matthew 5:27-30 . . . .**117**

Matthew 5:38-48 . . . .**75, 109**

Matthew 6:5-15 . . . .**95**

Matthew 6:6-8 . . . .**87**

Matthew 6:9-13 . . . .**99**

Matthew 6:26 . . . .**79**

Matthew 7:7-11 . . . .**72**

Matthew 7:15-16 . . . .**120**

Matthew 7:24-27 . . . .**125**

Matthew 7:24-29 . . . .**11**

Matthew 9:35-38 . . . .**45**

Matthew 10:32-33 . . . .**36**

Matthew 14:25-31 . . . .**48**

Matthew 16:1-4 . . . .**46, 86**

Matthew 17:20 . . . .**16**

Matthew 18:21-22 . . . .**37**

Matthew 19:3-8 . . . .**100**

Matthew 21:21-22 . . . .**42**

Matthew 22:37-40 . . . .**106**

Matthew 23:13-28 . . . .**76**

Matthew 25:1-13 . . . .**97**

Matthew 25:14-29 . . . .**124**

Matthew 25:32-46 . . . .**23, 95**

SCRIPTURE INDEX

Matthew 26:30-35	**108**	John 2:13-17	**104**
Matthew 26:40-41	**76**	John 3:16-18	**82**
Matthew 28:1-10	**42**	John 3:16-21	**45**
Matthew 28:16-20	**83**	John 4:22-24	**94**
Mark 4:22	**70**	John 7:24	**88, 91**
Mark 8:1-13	**116**	John 8:15-16	**91**
Mark 9:17-27	**93**	John 11:32-44	**42, 83**
Mark 10:45	**121**	John 13:3-16	**112**
Mark 11:25	**52**	John 14:1-3	**25**
Mark 14:10-11	**17**	John 15:5-8	**95**
Luke 4:16-30	**77**	John 15:12-13	**73, 79**
Luke 6:27-30	**18, 63**	John 20:24-31	**46, 48**
Luke 6:36	**76**	John 21:10-19	**108**
Luke 9:23-24	**36**	John 21:15-17	**62**
Luke 10:29-37	**21**	Acts 2:36-41	**71**
Luke 10:38-42	**26, 71**	Acts 2:42-47	**20, 25**
Luke 12:2-3	**76**	Acts 4:29-33	**21**
Luke 12:15-31	**63**	Acts 5:1-11	**102**
Luke 12:16-21	**55**	Acts 13:40-41	**116**
Luke 12:22-31	**86**	Acts 17:24-28	**58, 60, 78**
Luke 12:27-34	**80**	Acts 20:7-12	**83**
Luke 12:32-34	**93**	Acts 20:22-24	**56**
Luke 12:58-59	**30**	Acts 22:1-24	**48**
Luke 14:25-33	**36**	Acts 24:14-16	**71**
Luke 15:3-7	**49**	Romans 1:18-25	**44**
Luke 16:1-13	**120**	Romans 2:14-16	**64**
Luke 16:16-17	**18**	Romans 3:19-28	**129**
Luke 17:3	**101**	Romans 5:1-5	**23**
Luke 22:14-16	**121**	Romans 5:6-8	**73**
Luke 22:14-20	**65**	Romans 5:7	**105**
Luke 24:44-53	**116**	Romans 7:14-25	**89**

Romans 8:1-5 . . . . **117**

Romans 8:6-14 . . . . **117**

Romans 8:12-17 . . . . **67**

Romans 8:14-17 . . . . **10**

Romans 8:24-31 . . . . **92**

Romans 8:28 . . . . **92**

Romans 8:28-31 . . . . **34**

Romans 8:35-39 . . . . **106, 114, 128**

Romans 10:8-13 . . . . **106**

Romans 12:1-2 . . . . **22**

Romans 12:1-8 . . . . **31**

Romans 12:4-5 . . . . **25**

Romans 12:10-13 . . . . **25**

Romans 13:1-4 . . . . **103**

Romans 14:10-13 . . . . **88**

Romans 15:5-7 . . . . **25**

Romans 16:3-4 . . . . **123**

1 Corinthians 3:16-17 . . . . **84**

1 Corinthians 6:15-20 . . . . **114**

1 Corinthians 9:19-23 . . . . **101**

1 Corinthians 9:24-27 . . **24, 110, 118, 125**

1 Corinthians 11:3-7 . . . . **94**

1 Corinthians 12:4-10 . . . . **122**

1 Corinthians 12:14-31 . . . . **20, 58**

1 Corinthians 12:20-27 . . . . **21**

1 Corinthians 12:22-25 . . . . **83**

1 Corinthians 14:6-11 . . . . **101**

1 Corinthians 15:33 . . . . **53, 87**

1 Corinthians 15:52-57 . . . . **83**

1 Corinthians 16:13-14 . . . . **67**

2 Corinthians 1:3-7 . . . . **42, 100**

2 Corinthians 4:1-2 . . . . **44, 66**

2 Corinthians 5:1-3 . . . . **43**

2 Corinthians 5:14-17 . . . . **54**

2 Corinthians 7:8-10 . . . . **101**

2 Corinthians 12:8-10 . . . . **62**

2 Corinthians 13:5-6 . . . . **125**

Galatians 2:11-14 . . . . **25**

Galatians 3:9-14 . . . . **82**

Galatians 3:26-29 . . . . **27**

Galatians 5:16-18 . . . . **59**

Galatians 5:16-25 . . . . **51**

Galatians 5:22-23 . . . . **54**

Galatians 6:3-5 . . . . **32**

Galatians 6:9-10 . . . . **126, 130**

Ephesians 2:4-7 . . . . **101**

Ephesians 2:8-9 . . . . **81**

Ephesians 4:14-15 . . . . **85**

Ephesians 4:17-27 . . . . **27**

Ephesians 4:25-27 . . . . **12**

Ephesians 4:29 . . . . **30**

Ephesians 4:29-32 . . . . **99, 122**

Ephesians 4:31-32 . . . . **65, 130**

Ephesians 6:1-3 . . . . **87**

Ephesians 6:1-4 . . . . **71**

Ephesians 6:11-17 . . . . **14, 97**

Philippians 1:9-10 . . . . **11**

Philippians 2:3-4 . . . . **95**

Philippians 2:3-8 . . . . **98**

Philippians 2:14-17 . . . . **106**

Philippians 3:7-14 . . . . **34**

Philippians 3:17-21 . . . . **13**

SCRIPTURE INDEX

Philippians 3:18-21	**34**	James 1:27	**28**
Philippians 4:10-13	**32**	James 2:1-4	**43, 128**
Colossians 3:9-10	**77**	James 2:15-16	**118**
Colossians 3:9-11	**83**	James 2:17-24	**21**
Colossians 3:11	**97**	James 3:3-12	**122**
Colossians 3:11-14	**27**	James 3:5-10	**99**
Colossians 3:12	**44**	James 4:17	**64**
1 Thessalonians 1:6-7	**91**	1 Peter 1:3-9	**48**
1 Thessalonians 5:1-6	**55**	1 Peter 1:6-9	**93**
1 Thessalonians 5:4-8	**22**	1 Peter 2:9-11	**115**
1 Thessalonians 5:11	**67, 99**	1 Peter 3:3-4	**111**
1 Timothy 2:9-10	**85**	1 Peter 3:8	**110**
1 Timothy 3:7	**91**	1 Peter 4:8-10	**110**
1 Timothy 5:8	**99**	1 Peter 4:10-11	**20, 122, 125**
1 Timothy 6:6-8	**19**	1 Peter 5:8-10	**107**
1 Timothy 6:9-11	**40, 99**	2 Peter 2:1-3	**81**
2 Timothy 1:6-7	**16**	1 John 1:6-10	**29**
Titus 2:11-14	**57, 109**	1 John 2:15-17	**81**
Hebrews 3:17	**53**	1 John 3:1-10	**24**
Hebrews 4:13-16	**108**	1 John 3:16-18	**21, 69**
Hebrews 5:11-14	**118**	1 John 4:16-19	**10**
Hebrews 10:10-14	**129**	Revelation 3:20	**72**
Hebrews 10:23-25	**18**	Revelation 19:6-9	**73**
Hebrews 10:32-36	**12**	Revelation 22:16-19	**18**
Hebrews 11	**65**		
Hebrews 11:1	**92**		
Hebrews 11:1-13	**16, 34**		
Hebrews 12:5-11	**37**		
Hebrews 12:14-15	**52**		
James 1:2-4	**91**		
James 1:13-15	**33**		
James 1:19-20	**93**		

TOPICAL INDEX

Abortion 10

Absent Father 10

Absolute Truth 11

Abuse 12

Accountability 12, 41

Addiction 13

Adultery 100

The Afterlife 23

Aliens 78

Anger 14, 56, 65, 93

Animals 45, 93

Appearances 89

Armor of God 14, 97

Assurance 106

Authenticity 15

Authority 16, 103

Belief 16, 42, 46, 116

Betrayal 17

The Bible 18

Bitterness 52

Blame 103

Body Image 19, 111

The Body of Christ 20, 58

Boldness 21

Boundaries 115

Bullies 21, 84

Busyness 26

Change 22

Character 23

Cheating 18

Choices 23, 56, 96

Christianese 101

Christ-Likeness 24, 91

Church 18, 25, 130

Cliques 25, 128

Cloning 26, 31

Comfort 42

Communication 27

Community 20, 25, 27

Compassion 28, 44, 110

Competition 110

Complaining 29

Confession 29

Confidence 16, 34

Conflict 30

Conformity 22, 31

Confrontation 101

Consequences 97

Contentment 19, 32

Counsel 44

Courage 32

Creativity 14, 34

Curiosity 33

Dancing 15, 34

Death 34, 83

Deceit 39, 128

Dedication 35

Denying Christ 36, 108

Desires 59

Discernment 11

Discipleship 36

Discipline 10, 37, 38

Dishonesty **38**

Disobedience **33, 38**

Distrust **39**

Divorce **100**

Doubt **39**

Dreams **40**

Drunkenness **40**

Duty **41, 106**

Easter **42**

Elijah **42**

Encouragement **42, 67, 99, 122**

Enemies **18**

Equality **43, 62, 83, 112**

Ethics **44**

Euthanasia **44**

Evangelism **45**

Evidence **46**

Expectations **46, 77**

Facades **47, 67, 102**

Faith **16, 48, 93**

Faith Sharing **48**

False Prophets **120**

Family **22, 49, 99**

Fathers **58**

Favoritism **50, 128**

Fear **51, 66**

Flesh vs. Spirit **51, 117**

Forgiveness **37, 52, 63, 75**

Free Will **53**

Friends **53**

Fruit of the Spirit **54**

The Future **55**

Generational Sin **56**

Generosity **56**

Gluttony **40, 57**

God **58, 62**

God's Family **25, 58**

God's Guidance **59**

God's Love **10, 53, 60, 127**

God's Omniscience **60**

God's Power **32**

God's Ways **48**

Good **92**

Gossip **61, 122**

Grace **62, 72, 108**

Grades **62**

Gratitude **29**

Greed **40, 63**

Grief **13**

Habits **118**

Happiness **63**

Heaping Coals **75**

Heaven **25, 34, 43**

Helping Others . . **21, 64, 69, 72, 95, 105**

Heroes **65**

The Holy Spirit **65**

Holiness **129**

Honesty **29, 66, 85**

Hope **67, 92**

Humanity **60**

Identity **67**

Image **102**

TOPICAL INDEX

Impatience	**19, 68**
Indifference	**118**
Influence	**23, 67, 69**
Inheritance	**34**
Injustice	**69, 104**
Inner Life	**70**
Integrity	**44, 71, 76, 119**
Jacob	**79**
Jesus	**71**
Jesus' Invitation	**72**
Jesus' Love	**73, 114**
Jesus' Sacrifice	**73**
Jonah	**97**
Joseph	**50**
Judas	**17**
Judging	**88**
Justice	**64, 74**
Kindness	**75**
Lazarus	**42, 83**
Leadership	**53, 76**
Learning	**51**
Legacy	**40**
Legalism	**76**
Lies	**29, 47, 71, 77**
Life	**78**
Listening	**78, 87**
Loneliness	**79**
Lost Sheep	**49**
Love	**73, 79**
Marriage	**73**
Materialism	**80, 81, 99**
Meaning	**63**
Media Messages	**19, 81**
Mental Illness	**81**
Mentor	**68**
Mercy	**37, 76, 82, 101**
Miracles	**83, 86**
Missions	**83**
Mistakes	**84**
Modesty	**85**
Music	**85**
Needs	**80, 86**
New Life	**54**
Noise	**87**
Non-Christians	**45**
Obedience	**87**
Obesity	**88**
The Occult	**33**
Omission	**64**
Oppression	**74**
Pain	**89**
Parents	**71, 89**
Participation	**21**
Patriotism	**27**
Peace	**85, 90**
Peacemaker	**109**
Peer Pressure	**27, 87, 120**
Perception	**91**
Perfection	**91**
Perseverance	**92, 125, 127**
Pity	**93, 104**
Pornography	**70**

Possessions 93

Praise Music 94

Prayer 95, 116

Prayer Requests 95

Predestination 96

Prejudice 97

Preparation 55, 97

Pressure 47

Pride 41, 46, 98

Priorities 99, 126

Put-Downs 30, 99

Questions 127

Racism 27, 83

Rape 74

Redemption 82

Regret 114

Rejection 28, 100

Relevance 101

Repentance 101

Reputation 91, 102

Respect 103

Responsibility 11, 103

Riches 120

Righteous Anger 12, 104

Risk 48, 105, 123

Romance 73

Sacrifice 36, 56, 65, 105, 106, 121

Salvation 106

Satan 107

Second Chances 62, 108

Secrets 70, 108

Self-Control 14, 57, 109

Self-Esteem 110

Selfishness 98, 110

Selflessness 95

Self-Worth 32, 79

Sensitivity 111

Serving Others 20, 112, 125

Sex 113

Sexism 113

Sexual Boundaries 113

Sexual Intimacy 114

Sexual Purity 115

Shame 36, 108

Sharing Faith 116

Siblings 128

Signs 116

Sin 33, 81, 117

Sin Nature 51, 89

Smoking 84

Sodom and Gomorrah 118

Spiritual Disciplines 24, 118

Stagnation 35

Standing Firm 67

Standing Up 118

Stealing 119

Stereotypes 91

Stewardship 120

Substance Abuse 120

Substitution 121

Success 99

Talents 122, 124

TOPICAL INDEX

Taming the Tongue **30, 61, 99, 122**

Teamwork **12, 123**

Temptation **76, 113, 117, 124**

Temptation of Christ **125**

Testing **125**

Time **126**

Tradition **94**

Tragedy **55, 107**

Trials **125, 127**

Trust **127**

Truth **38, 128**

Unconditional Love **128**

Uniqueness **79, 122**

Unity **90**

Witnessing **71**

Works **21, 81, 129**

Worship **69**

Wounds **130**